DATE DUE

OC 5 '01			

DEMCO 38-296

LOSS AND GRIEF RECOVERY:

Help Caring for Children with Disabilities, Chronic or Terminal Illness

Joyce Ashton
Lewisville Medical Center Hospital, Texas

with Dennis Ashton
Director Private Social Service Agency, Texas

Baywood Publishing Company, Inc.
AMITYVILLE, NEW YORK

BF 575 .G7 A7848 1996

Ashton, Joyce.

Loss and grief recovery

:ion Data

Ashton, Joyce.
  Loss and grief recovery : help caring for children with
disabilities, chronic, or terminal illness / Joyce Ashton, Dennis
Ashton.
     p.   cm.
  Includes bibliographical references and index.
  ISBN 0-89503-138-8
  1. Grief.   2. Bereavement—Psychological aspects.   3. Children—
Death—Psychological aspects.   4. Loss (Psychology).   5. Care of the
sick.   I. Ashton, Dennis, 1950-   . II. Title.
BF575.G7A7848   1996
155'9'37- -dc20
                                                         95-40492
                                                         CIP

DEDICATION

Cameron Dale Ashton

If I Had A

Wish

If I had a wish I would wish that I could walk! I would run and play and all the girls would like me. See it's hard to be handicapped in some ways. Like you can't do your homework without someone helping you. Sports would be fun to do, and I would play basketball. And I wouldn't miss standing in my prone stander if I could walk!

In some ways not walking is good luck because you get to drive early! (my wheelchair) And you don't even have to have a license. You also have a computer all to yourself. My wish will come true -- in the next life!

*by
Cameron Ashton*

Preface

When Dennis and I married we were happy, carefree, and innocent to life's tragedies. We faced each day with a determination to accomplish goals and make our dreams come true. We both finished college: I graduated as a registered nurse and Dennis with his bachelor's degree in psychology and master's degree in social work. We had faith in ourselves, our future, and our God.

We wanted a large family and were disappointed when infertility became part of our lives. When we finally conceived, our daughter Joyce D. was born nine months and two weeks after a normal healthy pregnancy. However, she died sometime during labor the night before her birth—"STILLBORN."

Over the next ten years we had four sons: Darren, Cameron, Andrew, Brandon, and a daughter, Ashley. We experienced a miscarriage and various medical problems with each delivery, three of which were C-sections. We watched our children face various challenges including Attention Deficit Disorder (ADD), learning difficulties, and asthma. As a result of Cameron's difficult delivery, he developed cerebral palsy. He lived a happy, productive life for fourteen years.

With Cameron's diagnosis we lost our carefree days and some of our innocence. With his death we lost more innocence and some of our happiness. We have had to find new ways to strengthen faith in ourselves, our future, and our God. This book is about that journey and what we have learned. Our hope is to encourage others as they face their own personal challenges through life.

Acknowledgments

The task of researching and writing this book was an overwhelming challenge for me. Each day I would wonder where to start and what to write. I found it was only after intense thought and sincere prayer that I would get the insight and direction in which to proceed. Thus, I must give credit to my Maker and the assistance He allowed from beyond this world.

I am indebted to the many professionals in their fields. I have relied heavily on their knowledge, experience, and research. I have quoted many throughout this book.

I am grateful to Cathy Long and Peggy Benedict who saw a need for a grief support program at our hospital and have allowed me to be the facilitator.

I acknowledge the many clients, patients, and parents that have shared their grief and sometimes painful experiences with us. We have learned from them and quote many, with their permission.

I am thankful for a supportive husband, children, and friends who allowed me to isolate myself on many occasions to work at the computer, and who, with other close relatives, loved and supported me through my own grief.

To my professor father who taught me to seek knowledge, my mother who believed in me and taught me faith, and my sister who listened and comforted me through my darkest days.

To Jack Morgan who saw the potential "contribution" in our work and referred us to Baywood Publishing Company, where Stuart Cohen, Lorna Roher, and Bobbi Olszewski provided additional support and professional expertise.

I wish to thank my friend and great American Impressionist, Leslie Young for the Cover painting. Its title is Impressionistic Abstract. I feel it depicts Illness, Loss, and Grief Recovery beautifully. Leslie also did the illustration in Chapter 3, page 31.

Although I have compiled our material and written most of this book, I have relied heavily on my husband, Dennis. His professional expertise and experience, resource material, and editing have been very valuable. And of course without CAMERON, WHOSE LIFE AND DEATH IMPACTED US BEYOND DESCRIPTION, this book would never be!

Contents

Prologue 1

CHAPTER 1 3
Introduction: The Challenges of Our Numerous Losses

CHAPTER 2 11
Our Struggle with the Diagnosis

CHAPTER 3 25
Caring for Our Child at Home

CHAPTER 4 49
Building Self-Esteem and Self-Worth

CHAPTER 5 69
Recognizing and Managing Our Grief

CHAPTER 6 91
Reconciliation of Our Loss:
Adjusting, Accepting, and Healing

CHAPTER 7 109
Our Relationships: Marriage, Friends, and Family
(Other's Reactions to Our Loss)

CHAPTER 8 131
The Role of Spiritual Healing

CHAPTER 9 161
　Other Considerations

APPENDIX 175
　Resources and Organizations

About the Authors 183

Index 185

Prologue

Many of life's challenges bring us stress and grief. The purpose of this book is to first help you recognize and confront these challenges. Then help you identify steps to better cope and ultimately resolve grief and find wholeness.

The grief reaction is often similar for many diverse circumstances and situations. Although most of this book can help anyone through any type of loss, the book focuses heavily on caring for children with disabilities, chronic or terminal illness, dealing with the loss, and the recovery process.

In Chapter 1 we introduce ourselves and discuss many of our past losses. We also illustrate how the accumulative effect of several challenges can make life seem difficult.

In Chapter 2 we discuss our struggle dealing with the loss we felt when our son received his diagnosis of a disability/chronic illness. We discuss anticipatory grief and the loss felt during the diagnosis process, additional focus on grief and steps to recovery are covered in Chapters 5 and 6.

Chapter 3 offers practical home care suggestions for those caring for a child at home during chronic, terminal illness, or with disabilities.

Chapter 4 discusses ways we found to build our own and our child's self-esteem and self-worth.

Chapters 5 and 6 address the grief process and self-help tools for recovery. In addition we discuss helpful ways we discovered to manage our stress.

Chapter 7 discusses other's reactions to our grief and offers ideas for improving relationships. It includes suggestions for couples, families, siblings, friends, and relatives.

Chapter 8 offers thoughts on the role of spiritual healing and finding personal wholeness. A summary of near death research is shared and how we found ultimate peace and understanding.

Chapter 9 has ideas on education, hospitalization, medical cost, doctors, dealing with seizures, placing a child outside your home, and extra help surviving murder and suicide.

Joyce Marsden Ashton, RN
Grief Counselor

CHAPTER 1

Introduction:
The Challenges of Our
Numerous Losses

> In each person's life, much of joy and sorrow revolves around attachments or affectional relationships—making them, breaking them, preparing for them, and adjusting to their loss [1, p. 285].

I stared at the cold hospital gurney that held the body of my fourteen-year-old son. It was 1 A.M. and the doctor had just informed me, "Your son is dead." I was numb and could hardly breathe. As a pediatric nurse I had seen dead children before, but now my own son. How could this be? I kissed him on the forehead and his familiar scent warmed my nostrils. "Is it him, is this really him, lying here motionless—DEAD?" I wanted to run away, hide, or scream out, "This cannot be happening!" My mind was frantically trying to find answers for so many questions, "How can I turn back the pages?" "How can I undo this horrible event?"

I left the room and found Dennis who had been at Cameron's side all night and had watched helplessly as medical interventions failed to revive his son. We went outside where we held each other and I cried on his shoulder, asking, "Why?" "Why?" I wondered if I could really carry on. Would I have the strength to endure life without my beloved Cameron?

Life is a challenge! If you do not believe this, then it may be that you have not lived long enough! Circumstances, often beyond our control, happen to all who step upon this earth. Some of us may erroneously think adversity effects only those who make poor choices, do something wrong, or are not shrewd enough to prevent and avoid adverse situations. Although we can bring trials upon ourselves, the fact is, even when we are doing everything to the best of our ability, things can go wrong. Illness, disabilities, divorce, financial struggles, rebellious children, loss of home or job, abuse, unwed pregnancies, infertility, miscarriage, disappointments, and death are only a few of the trials that can bring deep feelings of pain, distress, and sorrow.

How do we cope with life's challenges? Where can we turn for help? How do we find the happiness and joy in our life when so many things seem out of our control? Why did this happen to me? What is the purpose of our struggle with life? Why don't our desires and wishes always come about? These are the kinds of questions we, and possibly you, have sought answers for.

This was not our first experience with loss and grief. We had experienced both unexpected losses and what society labels expected losses. We will share some of our losses as an introduction to ourselves and as an explanation of our current understanding; also a loss scale (Figure 1) can be helpful to see the cumulative effect of losses in one's life.

LOSS OF PARENTS–SUICIDE

Dennis's mother took her life with carbon monoxide fumes in her own garage. She had just turned fifty years old and left a crushed and bewildered husband to raise two teenage boys. We watched them struggle for years trying to pick up the pieces of their lives and find answers to the many complex and painful questions that seemed to elude them. (We discuss suicide more in Chapter 9.)

My own father died Christmas morning a few years later. He was sixty-one and we had traveled 700 miles to be with extended family and exchange gifts. He had gone to bed about midnight reminding us to, "Make sure Santa didn't forget to fill the kids stockings!" Four hours later mother called us to their room because he was breathing strangely. My husband and I knew CPR (cardiopulmonary resuscitation) and we began it immediately. We were shortly joined by my brother who was a senior emergency medical resident, also visiting from out of town for Christmas. The paramedics soon arrived and transferred my father to a nearby hospital. Yet in spite of all this quick medical attention, his heart refused to take over on its own. It was a painful and confusing Christmas morning for all of us.

Because I had known for years Dad's heart was bad, I thought I was somehow prepared for his death. I wasn't! I had no idea it could hurt so much to lose a parent. I've realized since that we are seldom really prepared for the loss of any significant person in our life. I have come to

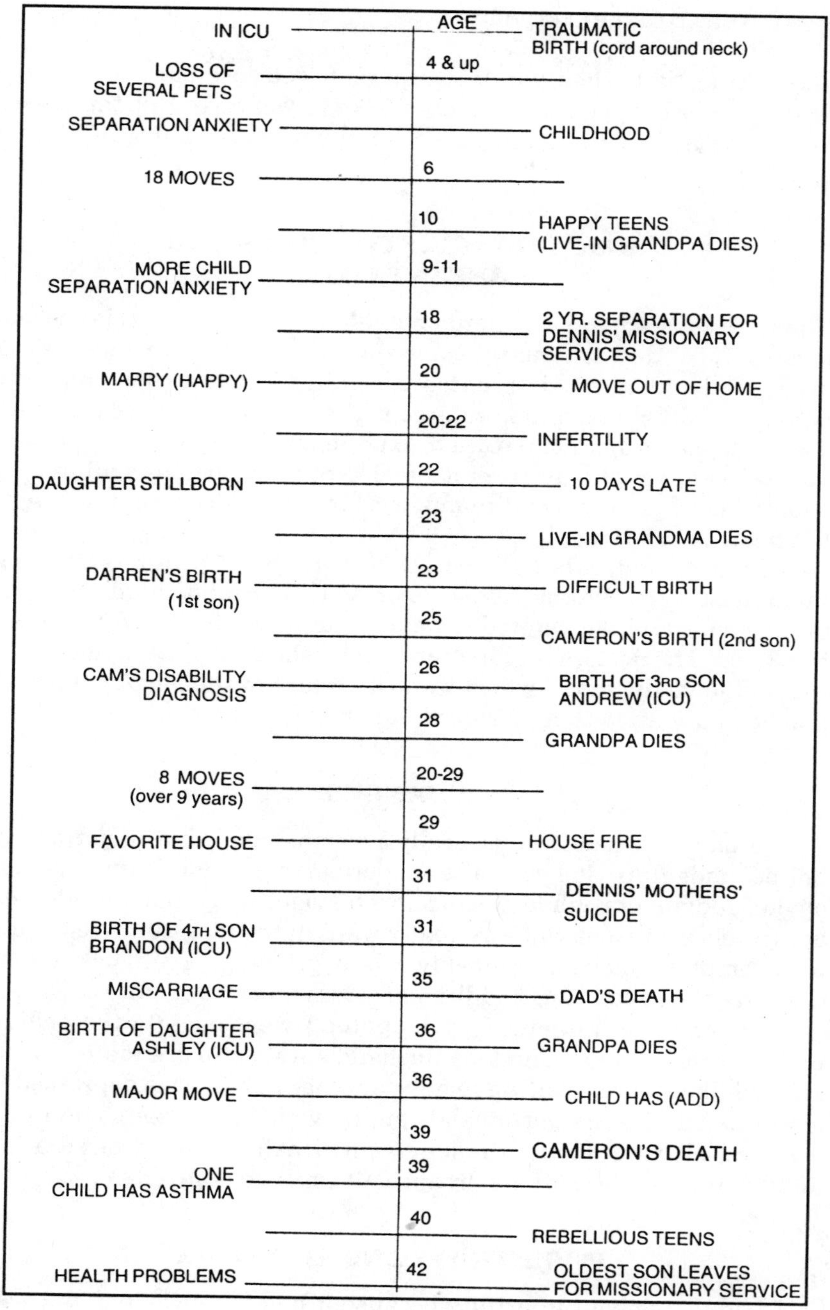

IN ICU ——————— AGE ———— TRAUMATIC
BIRTH (cord around neck)

LOSS OF —————— 4 & up
SEVERAL PETS

SEPARATION ANXIETY ——————————— CHILDHOOD

18 MOVES ———— 6

———— 10 ———— HAPPY TEENS
(LIVE-IN GRANDPA DIES)

MORE CHILD —————— 9-11
SEPARATION ANXIETY

———— 18 ———— 2 YR. SEPARATION FOR
DENNIS' MISSIONARY
SERVICES

MARRY (HAPPY) ———— 20 ———— MOVE OUT OF HOME

———— 20-22 ———— INFERTILITY

DAUGHTER STILLBORN ———— 22 ———— 10 DAYS LATE

———— 23 ———— LIVE-IN GRANDMA DIES

DARREN'S BIRTH ———— 23 ———— DIFFICULT BIRTH
(1st son)

———— 25 ———— CAMERON'S BIRTH (2nd son)

CAM'S DISABILITY ———— 26 ———— BIRTH OF 3RD SON
DIAGNOSIS ANDREW (ICU)

———— 28 ———— GRANDPA DIES

8 MOVES ———— 20-29
(over 9 years)

FAVORITE HOUSE ———— 29 ———— HOUSE FIRE

———— 31 ———— DENNIS' MOTHERS'
SUICIDE

BIRTH OF 4TH SON ———— 31
BRANDON (ICU)

MISCARRIAGE ———— 35 ———— DAD'S DEATH

BIRTH OF DAUGHTER ———— 36 ———— GRANDPA DIES
ASHLEY (ICU)

MAJOR MOVE ———— 36 ———— CHILD HAS (ADD)

———— 39 ———— CAMERON'S DEATH

ONE ———— 39
CHILD HAS ASTHMA

———— 40 ———— REBELLIOUS TEENS

HEALTH PROBLEMS ———— 42 ———— OLDEST SON LEAVES
FOR MISSIONARY SERVICE

Figure 1. Loss Scale.

5

understand that when you lose a parent, you lose part of your past. When you lose a spouse, you may feel as if you have lost the present. And when a child dies, you lose a large part of your future [2, p. 23; 3, p. 19].

MISCARRIAGE, STILLBORN, AND INFANT LOSS

We discovered that an infant or child's illness and death is one of the most painful and traumatic experiences a parent can have. We all expect and understand that parents usually die before their children. It is very hard for our minds to accept that our child has died first. It somehow seems against nature to experience this reversal. Society and nature have taught us to protect and provide for our children. We usually feel a great unconditional love for our children, that may not be felt in other relationships.

Our first child, a daughter, was stillborn. She was full term, weighing almost 7 lbs. Words cannot express how disappointed and heartbroken we were! We wanted to be parents more than anything else in the world! The doctors couldn't tell us why she died. (We struggled with the unknown diagnosis which we will discuss in the next chapter.) We reached forward with all our faith and hope to carry on.

CHANGES

We have learned it is generally recommended that major changes not be made until one year after experiencing a significant loss. Some of our judgments made during grief stages may not be sound, or accurately represent what we really want in the long-run. We tried not to attempt to move too quickly while grieving. Even positive and desired change can cause additional stress and confusion.

After the death of our first daughter I went back to the pediatric unit as a charge nurse, and my husband enrolled in graduate school. It seemed like forever waiting to have another baby. I was depressed and discouraged. We did get a small puppy which gave me something to love and nurture during the long wait! I had always desired a large family, and wondered if my dream could still be realized.

INFERTILITY AND ADOPTION

I had fears about infertility because it had taken so long to become pregnant with our first child. After she died, the loss and prospects of having to start all over again seemed overwhelming. Time seemed to move very slowly, each month seemed like an eternity.

Infertility can also be a challenge and a loss. Some couples may spend large amounts of time and money trying to conceive. They may look around, like we did, and wonder why everyone else makes it look so easy. We wondered, "Why us?," "What is wrong with us?," "What did we do wrong?," trying to find answers to questions that may or may not have solutions.

Some may choose adoption. While this brings joy and many lives are blessed by this process, remember even good changes can be stressful. Ambiguous feelings arise as the couple finally realize they will never have a child of their own making. Dennis has learned as an adoption worker that it takes time, work, and many adjustments after a couple receives a child.

A couple of years after the death of our daughter I was thrilled with the birth of a beautiful, healthy baby boy (Darren). Although I realized he could not take the place of our daughter, the joy I personally felt was beyond description. All of my dreams about motherhood were being fulfilled. I couldn't help but hurt and wonder about those who would NEVER experience this kind of love and joy. How would they cope? How would they totally resolve and reconcile their grief? I now felt content, life looked good to me again! Little did I know that our future held more challenges including more infertility, miscarriage, illness, and death.

LOSS OF RELATIONSHIPS– DIVORCE

After any loss, relationships with others may become strained. These are called secondary losses. Men and women grieve differently. More arguments may occur and couples may reject each other. Many parents find the grief and stress of illness and death so intense that they cannot support one another. We were surprised by the high divorce statistics after parents experience the diagnosis of a serious illness or death of their child.

The fortunate ones might find that they can stay close, often becoming a source of strength and support to each other. We have discovered this is possible if you are willing to work at it. In Chapter 7 we will discuss some specific steps to help your relationships survive and grow in the face of adversity.

MOVING

Research has shown that not only changing jobs, but changing living locations is high on the list of life's greatest stresses. Loss of identity and self-esteem may occur. It takes time and patience for many to adjust to a new situation or environment. Often children experience moving as a secondary loss following a death or divorce.

A year after the birth of our second baby my husband's work took us miles away from family, friends, and familiar support. We were lonely and homesick. We discovered that a move can be a loss and require many adjustments. We experienced some of the grief cycle again as we learned to adapt to our new surroundings in what felt like a whole new culture!

CHRONIC OR TERMINAL ILLNESS

Not many parents plan to deliver a baby that is not normal and healthy. No parent ever dreams their child will be diagnosed with a terminal illness. Few, if any are prepared for the new challenges they must face.

A year after our move I delivered another 7 lb. baby boy (Cameron). Only this time as the months passed we noticed he didn't progress developmentally as his older brother had. After several trips to our pediatrician, he suggested that a developmental screening be done. When Cameron was ten months old we received the official diagnosis of cerebral palsy. Although this was not classified as a terminal illness I knew the majority of these children do not make it to adulthood. I knew we were dealing with a chronic problem. I was shocked! Not us. I was a nurse, how had I missed noticing the signs? I remember closing all the drapes, taking the phone off the hook, and sobbing, "Why me?" I had already lost my first born, why another loss? Life was not fair! Life was too hard!

I learned that parents experience a variety of feelings when they discover their child is not "normal or healthy." Once again we found ourselves experiencing the grief cycle. It is normal for some to refuse to accept the diagnosis, or not even hear it initially. Denial may come in many forms. Some parents blame doctors and other professionals. I remember telling a therapist that I knew Cam would walk because he was so determined! (However, he spent all of his 14 years in a wheelchair.) I also assumed we would be one of the minority to see him grow into adulthood. Once again we reached and pulled for all the faith, hope, and strength we could find. Our parents, family, friends, and doctors lived many miles from us. Although they sent comfort and support through letters we had to find many new support systems to help us.

I was overwhelmed at how much I felt I needed to know about my child's diagnosis. I went to the library for information on how to help him or some self-help book on helping our lives become more manageable. I couldn't find much. I was determined then that when I learned what I needed to know, I would write this book in hopes of helping others not feel as lost as I did. (Unfortunately for 15 years I found I was too busy caring for Cameron and his siblings to do much writing.)

LOSS OF A CHILD

When the disabled, chronically, or terminally ill child dies, the pain continues for those left behind. Losing a loved one that was dependent on you can increase your grief reaction. The large amounts of invested time and energy can create irreplaceable relationships and may complicate your grief recovery. The loss of purpose and meaning may create enormous change in your life. We will discuss this in detail in Chapters 5 and 6.

Although Dennis and I were both professionals working with people who were experiencing loss, when we found ourselves enduring intense personal grief over and over, we realized we had only understood intellectually. Emotionally we were shocked at the enormous pain loss can bring. As time passed we were also surprised at the lengthy duration of our grief.

Now both of us have become more involved with grief issues. We speak on many related topics including adoption, abuse, infertility, stress, anxiety, depression, marriage, effective parenting, self- esteem, caring for disabilities, chronic, and terminal illnesses. Our primary focus and suggestions deal with loss and grief recovery.

We have experienced how loss and life's challenges may affect people very differently. For example, we found it confusing that it seemed easier for me to cope and deal with my mother-in-law's suicide than it was when we lost much of our home to fire! We have come to realize not only how complex life can be, but also how our own reactions to similar circumstances are very individualized. We've learned that many factors contribute to our views and our ability to recover from loss. The time, service, commitment, and emotional investment we give prior to a loss may intensify and prolong our grief reactions. I finally realized I had sacrificed and invested more emotionally to my home and family at the time of our fire than I had to the relationship with my mother-in-law who lived 700 miles away.

The pain of loss has taught us many things. We hope to share this knowledge and the comfort we discovered with others who are hurting and wondering if life really is worth living. We are not attempting to compare our pain to yours, because each person's personality, life experience, and situation is unique to them. There are many circumstances, factors, and attitudes that shape our experiences, and it is usually not valuable to compare our challenges. Yet, it is by sharing our unique challenges that we bond, identify, and eventually help each other resolve pain. Come now, walk with us for awhile. We can hold each other's hand, cry, and hopefully find the strength, peace, and comfort necessary to endure any loss (see Table 1).

Table 1. Kinds of Loss

A. LOSS OF POSSESSIONS (usually replaceable) keys and wallets, financial, important papers, homes, cars, natural disasters, fire, etc.	B. LOSS OF RELATIONSHIPS children leave/rebellious, infertility/miscarriage, pets, friends, deaths, separation/divorce, etc.
C. LOSS OF SELF (IDENTITY) change of lifestyle, divorce, loss of home or work, disabilities, illness, retirement, addictions, abuse, deaths, loss of body part, etc.	D. LOSS OF CONTROL aging/health, abuse, infertility/miscarriage, other's bad choices, suicide/murder/death, addictions/divorce, etc.

SECONDARY LOSSES
(LIFE DIDN'T QUITE WORK OUT AS WE'D PLANNED!)
loss of self-esteem, loss of plans, goals, dreams, and future

REFERENCES

1. K. A. May and L. R. Mahlmeister, *Comprehensive Maternity Nursing* (2nd Edition), J. B. Lippincott, Philadelphia, 1990.
2. H. Schiff, *The Bereaved Parent*, Penguin, New York, 1978.
3. P. H. Dunn and R. M. Eyre, *The Birth We Call Death*, Bookcraft Inc., Salt Lake City, Utah, 1976.

CHAPTER 2

Our Struggle with the Diagnosis

Receiving a diagnosis for a disabled, chronically, or terminally ill child is a major loss. For some, the struggle starts the day a child is born. "What do you mean something went wrong?" "What kind of complications?" Can I see or hold him/her?"

The birth of an ill or disabled child may happen suddenly and unexpectedly, often without preparation or warning. Or it may be weeks, months, or years before we understand an illness or receive a diagnosis. And many infants or children die without ever receiving a definite diagnosis. Our dreams become shattered into fear for our future.

THE UNKNOWN DIAGNOSIS

The day our first child was born was a day we'll never forget. She was ten days late and we were anxious for her to come! I had been in labor off and on for two days so we knew we were getting closer. When I woke up early that morning I didn't feel the usual movement and kicking inside me. I called my mother who is an R.N. (registered nurse) like myself, and told her about this lack of movement. She didn't seem overly concerned at first, yet proceeded to call a nurse friend of hers who worked in the delivery room. Her friend explained that some babies' movements can slow down during labor, however, it would be wise to go to the hospital and get checked. When I explained it all to my husband, it somehow confirmed his fears, that we may not get the baby we had awaited for so long!

When we arrived at the hospital the nurses could not hear any heart tones. They called our doctor who came quickly, however he couldn't find any signs of life either. He decided to break my water since I was in labor and had started dilating. The water (amniotic fluid) was green (meconium staining which means the baby had a premature bowel movement) and is a sign of stress. He then told us the baby had probably died during the night. We were shocked. I wanted to be a mother more than anything else. Now after two long years of trying and waiting I couldn't believe there would be no live baby. I felt so hopeless, telling the doctor, like so many do, "Just put me out and take it!" However, this is not the safest way, so I like many bereaved mothers, proceeded with the long hard work called labor. It was intensely discouraging to be awake and feel the pain only to receive a lifeless baby in the end.

After several painful hours I delivered a baby girl. She was beautiful and looked perfect, yet lay lifeless and still. It was hard for us to comprehend she was really not alive. We desperately wanted a reason for her death, yet none was found. A diagnosis of death without a cause was difficult to comprehend. "What did we do wrong?" We were hurt, shocked, and sad, experiencing many grief symptoms.

Often, as was the case of our stillborn and later a miscarriage, professionals were unable to give a formal name or reason for our children's deaths. (Unfortunately this is very common with miscarriages and stillborn babies. Approximately 25% of all pregnancies are lost.) This was very confusing for us and seems to be for many parents we work with. We are taught such high regard for medical knowledge and technology, that it is a shock to our system to be told by our doctors, that they don't know why an infant is born with problems, or dies. Sadly, we then become part of a statistic. Hearing that death is common, normal, and that one out of four pregnancies does not result in a live infant, is not very comforting.

DELAYED DIAGNOSIS

Getting a diagnosis can take time. Knowing that something is wrong . . . yet not finding out just what it is can be very draining.

Life was looking pretty good again when our third child came into the world. (We had a healthy two-year-old at home who had brought us much joy after the sorrow of our first loss.) Cameron was born after thirty hours of hard labor. He was ten days overdue like our first child, however, the doctor had done several extra things to ensure his safety. All the tests had been normal, yet in the delivery room

Cameron's heart rate suddenly dropped below normal. The doctor hurried to get him out and a dark blue body emerged. He wasn't breathing, so the nurses and doctors tried to resuscitate him. He had green amniotic fluid like our first daughter and had aspirated some in his lungs. Soon he started to breathe and his color began to improve. They irrigated the meconium stool from his lungs and said, "He would be fine, and that this happens to many infants." [His apgar (birth health test) scores were poor.]

When I finally got to hold him several hours later he cried and cried. He was irritable, and it was very difficult to calm him down. We blamed it on his difficult delivery and all the irritating throat and lung irrigations. (At the time I didn't know that irritability can be a symptom of a damaged central nervous system, caused from lack of oxygen.)

The next morning I noticed small jerky movements and twitches. Because I was a pediatric nurse and had seen seizures before, I was worried. I let the doctors and nurses know what I was seeing. They gave me different reasons for his symptoms and assured me that he was fine.

When we took him home his irritability changed to exhaustion, he would sleep through some of his feedings and all through the night. He also held his tongue at the top of his mouth in an abnormal fashion. I would express my concerns and fears only to be reassured that he was fine. After a week or so he was more alert and feeding well. He became a handsome, healthy, chubby, happy baby that we all enjoyed. I let go of my fears for several months.

TESTING

The time, expense, and sorrow that sometimes goes into obtaining a diagnosis may be exhausting for everyone involved. Again, you may or may not find the answers you are seeking.

When Cameron was between four and six months old, he still could not roll over well. His muscle tone was (mildly) weak and floppy. He could not sit alone. Again I expressed my fears to the pediatrician. He agreed, yet explained to us that some babies are just slower and that we should be patient a while longer.

By nine months old there was not a great deal of change. Finally, the pediatrician referred us to a Regional Diagnostic Center for an evaluation. I remained concerned, but felt that if Cam did have any problems they would be resolved with time.

When Cam was ten months old a nurse specialist came to our home to do an evaluation. She watched his movements, how he reached for toys, his mid-line orientation, and general posture. She then told me he had some "motor delays." I thought okay, "delays," he can catch up. At the time I just could not understand what she was telling me. I asked her about any mental retardation which professionals sometimes call "delays," which means some developmental involvement. I showed her how he seemed to understand when I would say, "Cameron give me a kiss," and he would smack his lips together and then smile. She explained that his responses and bright alert mannerisms indicated that his intelligence could be normal, however, formal testing in that area would be done later. She was only testing his motor skills and they were definitely delayed. She said, "It was very hard to predict how much progress someone like Cameron could make." I was so confused! What was she telling me? She then asked me if she could watch him eat. He would bring food to his mouth, yet he was slow and sloppy. "Weren't all babies?" She pointed out that his chewing and swallowing were not normal. He had "tongue thrust" which caused him to push some of his food out as he chewed. I became increasingly anxious. I could feel the tears swelling up in my eyes as she showed me a way to hold his jaw. She explained that because his mouth was involved, I should offer him "oral support." What was she telling me? I bit my tongue to stop the tears from spilling down my face, revealing all my helplessness and fears. She then told me, "That speech delays can be a result of mental or motor damage." I managed to ask her how long I would have to do this jaw support? She said, "She knew a four year old who still needed it!" Four years, Wow! That was it, I knew I couldn't hide my emotions much longer! I hurried and helped her out the door. As she was leaving she let me know she would send someone back to go over some of the equipment Cam would need to start using!

I locked the door, took my phone off the hook, and put Cameron down to nap. Now I was alone. I finally let the tears come. I cried and cried, yet I still did not totally understand what the nurse had told me.

When I got somewhat composed I got out all my nursing books and tried to find something on motor damage. Slowly as I read, I began to put things together. I looked up several childhood illnesses and diagnoses and read the definitions. I found one section where there were several of the terms the nurse had used! I couldn't believe it, Cameron had cerebral palsy! Fear gripped me. The shock was overwhelming! I cried again with such despair. "Why me? I don't want this to be true. How can I ever raise a child with these kinds of problems?" I knew I wasn't strong enough and could not possibly endure such a challenge. In spite of all these feelings I still hoped (as many do) that if we worked hard, and had faith, we could catch up and overcome it all!

When my husband returned with our now almost three-year-old son, Darren, I explained all the nurse had said to me, and how I had come up with the diagnosis. He suggested I call her and confirm my conclusions in the morning.

When I called her, she explained that a doctor needed to give the formal diagnosis, however in her mind, her findings had confirmed my diagnosis. (We could hardly believe that after enduring such grief and loss with our first child that we had to face another huge challenge with this child.)

Most of us are not taught skills in our youth about dealing with loss or an abnormal diagnosis. Like myself, many little girls (and some boys, like Dennis did as a young child!) love to play with dolls. They feed and change them. They may think how much fun it would be to have a real baby. As they grow older they may even dream about the kind of children they might have, what they would look like, and the kind of life they will enjoy together. These plans, hopes, and dreams do not usually include caring for disabilities, terminal illness, or infant and child death.

Most parents, like us, will experience part or all of the grief cycle with each loss. Their hopes and dreams are gone, or at least must be changed. Such a loss may bring intense uncertainty about your entire existence.

PROFESSIONALS

It is also difficult on professionals when they cannot determine a reason for a disability, death, or illness. They also want to find all the answers available, and when they do not, they too feel confused and often inadequate. My husband and I have been in both positions. It is difficult to offer comfort or be comforted.

Often as the caretaker, we have nowhere to put our anger, but upon the professional. I know this is a common occurrence for many parents. We all have doctor stories and could share our frustrations in how and when we received our diagnosis.

It is necessary for our own survival to dump our anger someplace. We're mostly angry because our children are not whole (professionals seem to be the focus) [1, p. 117].

Parents may sense, even before the professionals, that something might not be right with their child. Even when everything looks normal, and the doctors assure you that all is normal, you just feel worried.

It is common for all parents to worry about their children. However, when parents actually find out the baby or child that they have learned to love so dearly has something wrong, it is intensely painful.

The joy we had planned to experience was replaced with worry, fear, and guilt. Again we wondered, "What did we do wrong?" "What do we do now?" "Where is the cure?"

Some parents may immediately sense society's negative labels and attitudes through nurses, doctors, friends, and family. They may feel lost at what to do or feel themselves.

It is also common for professionals to delay giving a diagnosis. They have fears too . . . "What if they are wrong?" "How will the parents handle the news?" Often professionals will document an illness in their notes long before the parents are actually told. Many times the parents finally say, "Please just tell us what is wrong." We had gotten to this point and so had one of our friends. Her daughter's name was Stacy. Over the years I have heard the same scenario many times.

Stacy was a premature infant who went to the ophthalmologist for a recheck. He had told them two months before that he didn't think there was optic (eye) damage from the high oxygen level that premature infants sometimes need while in the intensive care unit. But today he said, "He had suspected it two months ago and now he was sure . . . she was blind." In shock, her parents ask what they could do to help her. The doctor said, "Give her lots of love, handling, and sensory input." He offered no referrals for help and didn't mention knowledge of any infant stimulation programs. It was months later, after their own research this family found a program and therapy. Fortunately in their area it was cost free from birth on for developmentally delayed infants.

FACING THE FACTS

Finally when a diagnosis is given, it can bring some relief. At times the shock can be overwhelming, however, not knowing can also make it difficult for us to move toward helping ourselves or our child.

Listen to the feelings of a mother I spoke with trying to face the fact of her child's diagnosis realistically. She is writing in her journal to her two-year-old daughter who recently died accidentally. She is also the mother of a mentally-emotionally disabled child who is about eight years old.

> I have big, big problems this week! I had a special blood test done and it shows that I have a high chance for having a "Downs" with this pregnancy. I'm sick, I'm scared, I'm bitter. Why couldn't the

test be normal? My soul is in an awful state. I will have to have another test to determine what is wrong. This test, an amnio, is very accurate. If this baby is "Downs" what will I do? I can't possibly raise another child with problems I have so many of my own personal problems with stress, ulcers, etc. . . . and Ryan with such time consuming problems. His problems are just getting worse and worse. He is harder and harder to handle and to figure out. I have accepted that. I will do my best to raise him. Your death I will never truly handle. You don't know how it has crippled me. I cannot raise a "Downs" child. Can I? But what else can I do? Abort it? Could I live with that? Would I ever be able to be forgiven? Give the child up? How could I live with that? How can I explain these things to anyone? NO ONE KNOWS MY PAIN. Help me Lord, Help me Christ, Help me my daughter, give me peace. Let me know, let this baby be normal, please, please, please!! Love Mom.

One can feel the inner struggle and sorrow this diagnosis brings to this mother. Also the accumulative effect of three losses. The heart wrenching decisions that many parents wrestle with are often beyond our comprehension.

Another mother of a child with cystic fibrosis (lung disease) shared with me similar emotions as she had to face the facts.

The hunger for knowledge is really overwhelming, but the answers are sometimes a rude slap in the face. . . . It has made me not really want to know some of the answers to my questions. When we were first diagnosed, I read everything and one day Travis was pretty sick (difficulty breathing) and I went to my "C. F. handbook" for comfort. To my regret no comfort was found, I read that the lung problems were what killed the C. F. patient.

She discovered as we had, that you need some form of comfort and hope to get through the days and years ahead.

When hope is gone, what is left? Hope is sustenance; hope is a vital commodity; hope is the fluid of life itself [2, p. 144].

There are resources we found listed throughout this book that were helpful to us. Friends, family, and even professionals can offer honest hope and support. Many feel others, especially professionals appear cold, uncaring and too busy to offer the support they need. How comforting it could be if they could say something like this, "I am very sad and hurt your child has a disability or terminal illness. I realize this is shocking news and you may need time to be alone. I'll call you later and we can meet and discuss your concerns, fears, and questions. Maybe I can help you as you make plans for your future." Dennis and I were especially comforted by the words, "I'll be here for you as long as you need me."

ANTICIPATORY GRIEF

A variety of feelings will surface when you learn a child is not expected to live a long healthy life. It is a real loss, and you may feel lost, helpless, and out of control. Although much of the grief cycle may be experienced before death, that grieving may be different when a child dies suddenly. You may begin anticipatory grief, which facilitates one's acceptance of the reality of the diagnosis and ultimate impending death, gradually. You still have your child, yet you often don't know for how long. It is frightening and painful for parents to lose their dreams for their child's future. You may become angry and strike out, even to those you love the most. One mother said,

> I seem to be stuck in the steps of acceptance. Guilt because I couldn't fix it. Anger because it happened out of my control. Depression because of both the above mentioned reasons. I am being treated for a "situational depression" and I am on medication. I don't believe I could function without it. Some of my family doesn't believe this medication is good, and look down on it. But it helps me cope with the day to day. It also helps me sleep, which I don't need much of.

Others are angry at the child, and then feel guilty for their anger because they know it's not their child's fault they're ill or dying. It can be a vicious cycle. Some blame doctors and other professionals. One mother was angry because she felt her doctor had ignored all her concerns long before the diagnosis process began.

One needs to be careful that the anticipatory grief is not so effective that the parents withdraw emotionally from the child before the actual death occurs.

DENIAL

We may refuse to accept the diagnosis, or not even hear it. Denial comes in many forms. I remember telling a therapist when Cameron was about eighteen months old that I just knew he would learn to walk because he tried so hard and was so determined. I wasn't ready then to learn my child would spend the rest of his life in a wheelchair! I have seen similar denial in others, and relate well to Pearl Bucks comment,

> Driven by the conviction that there must be someone who can cure, we take our children over the surface of the whole earth, seeking the one who can heal [3, p. 17].

It often takes a long time for parents to fully realize the extent of their child's illness. Many may spend their lives seeking for a cure that simply does not exist. While parents can seek out the best possible services, they must strive to maintain realistic goals to avoid disappointment and discouragement. A good professional can guide parents through this search and help them work through their denial.

Occasionally a parent remains in true denial until the child dies. One mother told me,

> I am still in denial of my child's cystic fibrosis. I tell the doctors that one day they'll do his sweat test and it will be negative. There are times when I feel that I would sell my soul to cure him. Money is not the issue. I ignore the diagnosis in a way, in order to get through a day without depression and tears. Going through the daily steps without thought becomes second nature.

We've discovered miracles can happen, however, they are the exception. We found nature usually takes it's course. (We will discuss faith, spiritual injury, and growth in Chapter 8.)

I spent a lot of time and money on physical therapy. At times Dennis questioned the overall lasting effects of this investment. While much of it did benefit Cam, and I wanted him to be the best he could, I did have some unrealistic expectations. This contributed to my denial.

SOCIAL WITHDRAWAL

It is common to socially withdraw after receiving a diagnosis. Some parents may simply lack the energy to explain the details over and over. When you do tell them, you may find some of your fears are realized. It is often hard for others to understand all you are experiencing when they have not encountered illness, disabilities, or death before. It may feel as though you don't have as many things in common with your friends and relatives. We, like many, were not sure how to tell friends or relatives for fear they wouldn't accept or understand the situation. Many said they had suspected something was wrong with our child, which only made us feel worse.

We became very busy with doctors, tests, and treatments. We found everything takes so long to do for your child. You become so tired that there doesn't seem to be much time for anything else. At times I had to push myself to go anywhere. Cameron was difficult to load into the car, my other children seemed impatient, and on three different occasions I had nursing babies that were screaming to eat! One mother describes our feelings well,

> All I wanted was a baby and now I've got doctors' appointments, therapy appointments, surgeries, medical bills, a strained marriage, no more free time . . . [4, p. 15].

Many children are too ill to get out much. You may worry others will pity you and your child. You may fear your child will look repulsive, or offend someone. Any of these feelings can encourage you to stay at home and avoid the emotional trauma you may encounter.

We found a lifetime of transitions and adjustments. We found if we were patient with others and tried to educate them as to what we were experiencing and needing, they could then help us cope and accept our situation and future better.

RELATIONSHIP CHANGES

Marital stress is common when a child becomes terminally ill or disabled. Many couples find the stress is so great they reject the child, others, or each other. More arguments may occur during the shock and adjustment stages. Having an ill child can add stress to your marriage, however it's not the child himself that causes the marriage problems. When couples cannot communicate, deal with their feelings, or make a plan for their life (with this new challenge), conflicts may come. We learned a good marriage is not without conflict, it is one where the couple has learned to deal with the conflict. We also found ways we could draw closer and become a source of strength and support to each other as we worked through tough issues. We will discuss these techniques in greater detail in Chapter 7.

Siblings seem to be affected by the diagnosis and illness in a variety of ways. They may need help in understanding the diagnosis at their age level. Then they can form ideas on how to answer their own and their peer's questions. We found a two- or three-year-old child may begin to notice differences in others, yet is very accepting. About age four or five they will want the "how" and "why" questions answered. Elementary school age children will be very curious and fearful about disabilities and illnesses. They may fear, "Will this happen to me?" We discovered teens are often embarrassed by a sibling's illness, disability, or appearance. They too, may have real fears about their future. Openness and honesty are important. Let them know you have fears too. Do your best to be emotionally sensitive to THEM as well as their ill sibling.

IDENTIFYING SERVICES

When you first suspect a problem or receive a diagnosis, contact your local school district, County Health Department, hospital, or doctor. They should be able to refer you for an appropriate evaluation. If you are not satisfied with a test or diagnosis, seek a second opinion. If the second doctor tells you the same thing, try to work through any denial and accept the help, advice, or referrals they may recommend.

After finding out Cameron would not lead a normal life, I had a great desire to find out everything I could. I asked doctors, nurses, social workers, and therapists many questions. The hardest thing I learned was that there were no sure answers to many of my questions, just guesses. No one could predict what Cam would be able to do or how long he would live. I even visited Special Education classes of older children to see what teens might look like with different problems. I found a large variety of symptoms and combinations. What would Cameron be like? I wanted to know and somehow control the unknown future of a child I loved so much.

Slowly over the years I was discovering what he would be like. I've learned the answers to most of my questions by watching and waiting. Many illnesses, disabilities, and conditions may be more clear cut than Cam's. You may be able to get more information about the future than we did. This will help you in deciding the appropriate services, equipment, and socialization for your child (see Chapter 3).

WHEN DO WE TELL THE CHILD?

Cameron's diagnosis became a part of his identity at an early age. He knew all the therapy was to help improve his abilities and life. He seemed to always know he was different than other children. We talked about it often. However, it took all of us several years to fully realize and accept all of his limitations and losses. It was a gradual process, some children may be faced with many losses all at once.

The age of the child being diagnosed is the main factor in the kind of information they receive about their illness or disability. It is generally recommended that they be informed by the parents, physician, or both within a twenty-four-hour period to avoid hearing it from someone else [5, p. 412]. Be as open and honest as possible. Know that children may have adult fears, but are unable to articulate them in adult ways. They may communicate nonverbally, symbolically, and with play or magical thinking (if I am really good the illness will go away) [5, p. 412].

ACCEPTING THE DIAGNOSIS

Once we realized we could not change the diagnosis of the child we loved, we were heading toward acceptance and healing. It did take time and patience. We still had setbacks and disappointments. One father described our feelings well,

> My philosophy of life is that it's like being on a beach. You get knocked down by a wave and you can either lie there and drown, or you can get up and move. If you don't keep moving you die [4, p. 8].

We believed as did Pearl Buck about her disabled child,

> . . . Only to endure is not enough. Endurance can be a harsh and bitter root in one's life, bearing poisonous and gloomy fruit, destroying other lives. Endurance is only the beginning. There must be acceptance and the knowledge that sorrow fully accepted brings its own gifts [3, p. 25].

Many parents, like us, looking back over the months or years can see their success. They are surprised that they have done so well. Many never thought they could do it. It wasn't easy, yet we made it! We, like many, learned to do more than just endure our situation. We were able to weave our child into our lives and find joy and happiness among the hardships.

We tried to see our son as a child first and as a chronically ill child second. It helped us to set proper priorities. Yes, he was different, yet we tried to focus on the positive, appreciating what he could do and how long he would be with us.

Christy Brown, a severely disabled child in "My Left Foot" said,

> If I could never really be like other people then at least I would be like myself and make the best of it [6, p. 137].

Once I had Cameron in the appropriate school, private therapy, and a home program, I drove myself into busyness. I sewed, cooked, gardened, mothered, hung wallpaper, and practiced nursing one day a week. These projects may have been considered "overactivity," however, they seemed to help keep my mind off some of my fears for his future. As I came to accept and understand what I could and couldn't do to help his condition and future, I became a calmer, happier mom, wife, and individual.

REFERENCES

1. F. Kupfer, *Before & After Zachariah,* Delacorte Press, New York, 1971.
2. L. Buscaglia, *The Disabled and Their Parents: A Counseling Challenge,* Charles B. Slack, Inc., Thorofare, New Jersey, 1975.
3. P. S. Buck, *The Child Who Never Grew,* Woodbine House, Bethesda, Maryland, 1950.
4. R. Simons, *After The Tears,* Harcourt Brace Jovanovich, Orlando, Florida, 1985.
5. T. A. Rando, *Grief, Dying and Death,* Research Press Co., Champaign, Illinois, 1984.
6. C. Brown, *My Left Foot,* Simon and Schuster, Inc., New York, 1970.

CHAPTER 3

Caring for Our Child at Home

Cameron did not receive a diagnosis until he was almost a year old. He was not considered "severe" and we felt we could handle any of his problems at home. We loved and enjoyed him so much. We, like many parents, did not consider anything other than keeping him in our home. Of course at this time we did not fully comprehend the vastness of his disabilities. He looked like "normal" babies his age, and it wasn't until a few years later that you could see his "differentness." He recognized us early on as an infant, and responded with normal anxiety upon separation when we left him. This and other observations indicated to the professionals that he probably had a "normal" intelligence, which is usually above 84. Borderline IQ is 71-84 [1, p. 296]. Mild retardation is in the 50-55 to 70 range, moderate retardation falls about 35-40 to 50-55, severe is 20-25 to 35-40, profound mental retardation is below 20 or 25 [1, p. 50]. However, more accurate testing would be done when he was older. (His later scores ranged from 78-110.) Although it was a lot of hard work, we are glad we were able to keep him at home. There were benefits for him and for our family. However, we realized that not everyone is able to care for their child at home. We will discuss Placements options in Chapter 9.

Once you have decided that you are able to care for your child at home, it is to your advantage to find all the resources available to help you. It will not always be easy, yet can be rewarding. Many "burn out" because they try to do it all without help and support. All parents need a break from parenthood to renew and recover. They need to take time to "Sharpen their Saw" [2, p. 47]. Just as you cannot continue to cut

25

wood with a dull blade, you must take time to stop and rest to work effectively.

This principle is especially true for those caring for disabled, chronically, or terminally ill children. There is usually more to do in one day than is humanly possible. You need to be able to leave your child in the care of someone else, even for brief periods of time. Not everyone can afford to hire help. You may have to be creative. You may have to ask friends, relatives, or other volunteers to help you. Take some time to think and write down ways you can "sharpen your saw" [2, p. 47].

SOCIAL NEEDS

Often socialization needs are not met for either parent or child. It may become easier to hide at home, with the curtains pulled, than to face the world. When a child is ill often everything and everyone is put on hold or ignored. One mother said she couldn't find support during the illness, she felt no one wanted to help her until after the death of her child. This is a real challenge for families. Another mother said,

> I am the main caregiver. My husband doesn't really do much of the necessary care. He has thrown himself into his work and earning the money to enable me to stay at home. This has caused some arguments because if he would give some of the medications, or treatments I could have a break, or eat hot food! (see Marriage Conflicts, Chapter 7).

One mother expressed what I, and others mothers feel:

> My doctor has said he wished there was a group of parents that could trade babysitting duties. When I think of that it scares me because I just don't know if they could take care of my child the way I do. Most of the time I feel I'm the only one that can do it. This is hard because it allows me no time for myself. Each time I've started an exercise class, he gets sicker and I feel I have to quit going.

If the child is in remission (a state of temporary recovery) parents are still afraid to socialize. They worry, "What if the child 'catches' something? What if going to the store, playground, school, or even family functions causes another flare up and puts them back in bed or the hospital?" Parents often feel they must watch everything so closely. They feel they must catch the first sign of illness hoping they can stop its progression. The relapses and remissions are difficult to cope with because of the confusing cycle of hope, disappointment, fear, guilt, anger, detachment, then hope again. The anticipatory grief cannot prepare them for all they will face.

If a child's disability also includes behavior problems that are difficult to control, parents may want to get out, yet find it difficult to leave them and almost impossible to take the child with them. One mother writes about her son's difficult illness and behavior. Her feelings are intensified after her two year old's death.

> I'm pretty miserable. I'm sad, I'm frustrated, I'm angry, and I'm trying to figure out what I have done so wrong in my life to deserve so many bad things. My son's behaviors are going from bad to worse. I can only be around him sometimes for an hour before he drives me nuts. He shouts, he says bad words, he slaps, hits, and throws things. What can I do for him? How can I help him, and me?

When a child is very ill or disabled, requiring treatments and medications, it may be exhausting to the caretaker. They may be up most of the night and still have work or other children to care for during the day. One mother said,

> One thing that is hard to accept as "normal" is the anger at being tied to schedules. I get so tired of giving medications and breathing treatments that sometimes I could just burst! I feel guilty when I feel this way. I've been told these feelings are normal, but it doesn't make them go away, or any of it easier to deal with.

OUTSIDE HELP

Hospice, home nursing, parent support groups, respite or foster care is available in most states, along with other services. These home support services are often encouraged by the states because they are less expensive and have some advantages for you and your child compared to total institutional or hospital care. Check with your insurance company, and state or county health departments. Also local doctors, schools, or parent groups are often helpful in locating the best people or services available to help you.

RESPITE OR FOSTER CARE

For many years I took disabled or terminally ill children into my home while their parents took a break. It is called respite care. Another name is short-term foster care. It is provided by many states to allow parents a break from continuous care. Sometimes care was for just a few hours. On other occasions a child would stay for several days at a time. It can also be done in your own home when the child may be too ill to move. I provided the care as well as used the help myself to provide the breaks I needed from home and continuous care of Cameron. I had always used babysitters with my other children, but these respite providers were more knowledgable about chronic or terminal illness. It can help families and the child realize that others can share in their care. It relieves some of the pressure knowing someone else can give treatments, put on braces, feed, dress, give medicine, provide transfers in and out of a wheelchair, or just give a back rub, and read a story to a bedridden child.

A relative could also offer this service with your encouragement. It is socially healthy for everyone involved including the child. When you return you may experience renewed energy, patience, and frustrations often melt away.

I was apprehensive about providing respite care when I was already struggling to raise my own child with chronic needs. However, I soon learned some valuable lessons. First it provided my son with friends who couldn't walk or talk well like himself. Second, it helped my other children see there were many special kinds of challenges in the world. There were those who looked and acted strange. Other children, because of medications had body odor. Some were heavily congested with drainage in their eyes, nose, or ears. Most drooled and weren't "potty trained." We even found ourselves uncomfortable eating with some of the children, yet accepted Cameron's messiness. We began to understand how others might struggle and react to the odd things about our own son.

Also by providing respite care I was able to experience what it was like to care for a variety of disabled, chronically, and terminally ill children. First, I would have them just come for a visit so the parents could show me how they handle their child. We would all become somewhat acquainted and comfortable. Soon I saw and felt what it was like to have a teenage boy (who wore size 11 shoes and weighed 200 lbs.) jumping on my bed because developmentally he functioned as a two year old. I also learned what it was like to have a child you could never turn your back on because he/she would run out your door and down the street not sensing any danger. I would be exhausted after a few hours, yet these parents provided care every day, sometimes for many months or years. For many of these parents it seemed impossible to continue the schedule, especially if they had other children. I came to appreciate my own struggles.

I cared for one little girl who could only lay in her infant seat and moan. She took all of her meals as liquid through a feeding tube. Her mother had four other children and it was difficult to take them anywhere, and meet all their needs. I watched this mother struggle with the decision after four years to place her child in a home where a nurse would care for her most of the time. Because of this child's disability, she showed little awareness of her environment, and adjusted very well to her new nurse. Her parents brought her home regularly. This was a state foster care arrangement.

Some children have a limited perception of their environment, and often do not recognize or cry when their parents leave. They will be happy with new, or many caretakers. It can, however, be extremely hard for a parent to let go of the total care for a disabled, ill, or dying child. It is often difficult to admit you need help, and still feel loyal to your child. Your child may have been the focus of your life. Even when it may be best for the child and your family, it can cause painful emotions and guilt. Remember you must find ways to "sharpen your saw" [2, p. 47]. Fern Kupfer describes their first break from her severely disabled child,

> We're doing what people do in ordinary life. You're doing the dishes, I'm mowing the lawn. But we feel so free. Without him to move from room to room waiting for the next cry. . . . We both have to work on not feeling guilty for enjoying, relishing even, what is only, after all, a normal life [3, p. 177].

INFANT PROGRAMS

Soon after Cameron's diagnosis I was introduced to an excellent infant stimulation team. They helped me understand normal growth and development and showed me some of the things Cameron had missed in his first months of life. We had the services of a physical, occupational, and speech therapist. We also had the assistance of a teacher, home activity consultant, nurse, nutritionist, and doctors. Cameron and I attended a program together twice a week for two hours. The physical and activity consultant came to our home once a week. Everyone was very informative and supportive. I have lived in other districts and states where less services were available. I have come to realize we were fortunate to have this early intervention. In one area I had to use our legal system to get an appropriate program. I learned with education, parents can become their child's best advocate. This can sometimes be an exhausting battle for parents if they disagree with their doctors, state programs, or school system. There are federal and state laws designed to protect the rights of children. We will discuss this more under education (in Chapter 9) which usually begins at age three, after the infant programs end.

FEEDING (EATING)

Many children lack the strength or coordination to sit up or even swallow well. In proper position it is much easier to use "jaw control" to feed them foods that were hard to chew or swallow. It is easiest done with the child on your lap, both of you facing the table. Your body supports the child's head and your left hand holds the chin, helping the mouth open and close. Your left middle finger is under the chin pressing up on the tongue. This technique of stabilizing the lower jaw can be used on premature infants, brain injured or weak children and adults (facing them) to help them not thrust so much food back out of their mouths [5]. We also found special spoons, cups, bowls, and plates which helped Cam feed himself.

EQUIPMENT

Depending on your child's illness you may find special equipment will aid in your child's care. There are many options on the market today for bathing, eating, positioning, respiratory aids, beds for sleeping, or help in sitting and mobility. (For detailed illustration and instructions, see [4].)

The week we got Cameron's diagnosis we received our first piece of equipment. The nurse that did our initial assessment came back the same week with a huge cardboard box. With knives and scissors she made a temporary "corner seat." Cameron had not been able to sit by himself because he lacked trunk control and balance. Therefore he had missed out on a normal ten month old's play. This chair would allow him to sit for longer periods of time because the corner and sides supported him. She made an "abductor wedge" with the other box corner which fit between his legs to keep his thighs apart and prevent his knees from rolling in (see Figure 1). This also prevented him from slipping and getting into an incorrect position. She even made a tray with the leftover cardboard. Now he could almost be like a normal ten month old who would be putting toys in his mouth and experiencing some oral stimulation.

She fixed his highchair too. She used "stocking net" (ropes or belts work too), to make peritoneal straps. She tied them onto the back of the

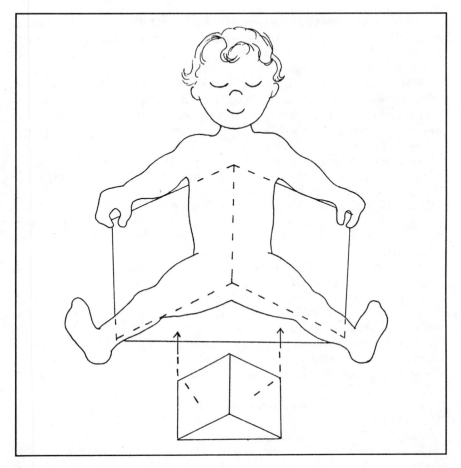

Figure 1. Corner seat.

highchair and brought them under and around his thighs in an X shape. Then she brought it behind his back and tied it. This held him very nicely in his highchair without slipping. Now Cameron would be able to sit and easily bring food or toys to his mouth without falling over or sliding through his highchair.

I learned that once you stabilize the lower trunk and body, the hands become free, rather than having to use them for balance. Now it wasn't so hard for him to feed himself. This was exciting. We used this technique for feeding, playing, coloring, and later for school and computer work. I was converted to the use and value of proper equipment. We soon had a permanent wooden corner chair that he used until he was twelve years old. It fit places his wheelchair wouldn't . . . like in a boat or sitting down on the sandy beach.

When Cam was between one and three years old he was easy to lift and handle. I had been given a home program by our physical therapist. We used large beach balls, bolsters, and wedges to perform movements he couldn't do alone. This equipment took up space, yet was valuable for increasing balance and strength.

By the time Cameron was three years old we owned several pieces of special equipment that he would rotate through, sitting, lying, or standing—thirty minutes in each. He had a prone stander which allowed him to be strapped standing upright. It also had a tray that he could eat, work, or play on. The standing allowed weight bearing which can promote bone growth, and prevent fragile hips from dislocating.

A wedge would allow him to lie on his stomach with his chest over the thickest piece and his hands on the floor for weight bearing on his arms. It also helped him lift his head up, strengthening neck muscles and facilitating head control. This exercise increased his muscle and joint strength in both arms and shoulders. It is also a nice position for newborns or children who often struggle or dislike being placed on their stomachs. A wedge can also offer relief from nausea or vomiting, by positioning a child's feet at the top and lying on his/her side [4, p. 33].

He also had a lightweight wheelchair similar to his corner chair. The legs could be elevated to stretch his tight hamstrings. This prevented contractures behind the knees.

Next to his electric wheelchair, his tricycle was his favorite piece of equipment. When he was three years old his physical therapist put velcro straps on the peddles of a small trike and tied Cam's feet on. What a thrill the day Dad came to school (as he did once a week to help with therapy) and watched Cam with great effort peddle the trike forward a few inches. It wasn't long before his legs became stronger and faster, then we were yelling, "Slow down!"

His electric bed allowed him to sit up on his own and made it easier to lift him from his bed to his wheelchair. An electric bed allows a very ill or weak child to sit up in bed to eat, read, or color.

We had a special rocking horse and rocking chair made so he could experience rocking movements. Both had special sides for support. We even made a floor scooter with wheels (prone crawler), so he could roll around lying on his stomach. This allowed him to experience movement and develop strength, as he explored from a normal baby's view.

Cam had most of the same equipment at school. His aides helped rotate his position throughout the day, and his dad and I tried to do it at home until bedtime.

TOYS

Toys often become a child's work and play. For the ill child, special toys have been developed to help them learn and grow in spite of their weakness. They may not have the strength, coordination, or fine motor skills to play with some of the regular toys.

I was always trying to make up for what Cameron couldn't do for himself. He couldn't get himself toys from the toy box like his brothers, so I was always handing him another toy when I felt he was finished with the previous one. We were very fortunate to have a toy library where we could check out different toys that were appropriate for special needs children. When we moved from that area I resorted to occupational catalogs for toy ideas (see Resources, p. 182).

VISION, HEARING, AND SPEECH

Your ill child may have a variety of needs. Once testing has been done, you, your doctor, and school administrators will have an idea of what special services are needed. When a child can see and hear their best, they will learn at a faster rate and their speech may also improve.

Cameron received speech therapy starting at one year of age. When he was older, not only did they work on the formation of correct sounds, but also his basic sentence structure. The spasticity in his tongue and lips made speaking hard work. He often would run out of lung capacity to complete a full sentence.

Speech can often deteriorate in very ill children, and to communicate they may use some simple sign language or a communication board.

I remember when Cameron got his first pair of glasses at age five. At first I thought he looked so funny. It wasn't long until I got used to them and thought he was adorable! I hoped the glasses could help him learn. He didn't need them long, and outgrew his astigmatism (abnormal curvature of the eye lens).

Hearing problems are often difficult to notice on an already disabled or ill child. However, formal testing is relatively easy. If you suspect a problem, request to have the hearing test performed. Hearing aids are small miracles, making a huge difference in many children's lives. Often children with hearing problems can attend schools or classes specialized for the hearing impaired. Another option is to provide an interpreter so the child can be mainstreamed.

HOME THERAPY

I learned in most instances the parents often become the primary therapists or caregivers. Most often it is the mother who nurtures and cares for the ill child. Even if she works outside the home, the first five years of most children's lives are primarily spent with their mother.

> If mother is despondent, tearful, disappointed, awkward, and wanting, so too, will be her husband and children [6, p. 77].

This notion places a lot of responsibility on mothers. She needs help! However, she can use this empowerment to influence and help her child and family. Christy Brown in the book, *My Left Foot* said,

> . . . Mother's faith in me seemed almost an impertinence. . . . She could not and would not believe that . . . though my body was crippled, my mind was not [7, pp. 10-11].

Many parents make great sacrifices to learn how to help their child. They often drive to schools or clinics to learn the tools that will help their child and themselves. Tonya Messingale remembers driving her daughter to doctors and therapy for two and a half years. She said,

> We felt all we did was get in our car and it automatically knew where and which direction to go.

I, too, felt an urgency to learn and understand all I could about my child's potential. Although I was a pediatric nurse, I had limited knowledge in developmental growth. I continued to struggle with the understanding that Cameron's brain was damaged in the motor areas and could not tell his body to move in the way it should. Normal infant movement and reflexes stimulate muscle and bone to develop properly. Because Cam's reflexes and movements were abnormal, this slowed down his muscle and bone growth. I soon realized that the short physical, occupational, and speech therapy sessions were wonderful, yet if I could carry over, and reinforce everything at home, even more progress might be made. I took this new realization seriously. Somehow it gave me hope for his future.

When he was small it was easy to do the exercises. I was taught simple range of motion movements to keep his muscles stretched and prevent contractures. (Contractures are permanent fixed muscles due to spasm or paralysis.) I tried to make it fun by doing some of his exercises on big balls or bolsters like his therapists did. I also tried to do a little routine everyday. This included changing his position and rotating him on different pieces of equipment. I tried to provide an occupational and speech activity as well as physical therapy each day.

Because I sensed I could make a difference in his life, I often became obsessed with organizing and implementing the "perfect" home program. I thought this would guarantee success in his progress and increase his life span. Of course this was unrealistic and soon I felt very overwhelmed.

Slowly I began to understand and gain some insights as to where and how I could help my child most. I learned to set priorities. I was able to adjust cognitively, my expectations, changing them as my family and I needed.

When he started a special pre-school at age three I felt we could slow down his home therapy some. We still faithfully pursued his P.T. (physical therapy). He received P.T. both at home and at school. In addition we took him once a week for private therapy. At about ten years of age, when he had reached most of his physical potential, we decided to let go of the private therapy. We then worked on transferring him in and out of his wheelchair and did exercises to maintain his flexibility and the little muscle strength he had. I do feel we made a significant contribution in aiding his physical progress. However, now I realize the relationship time was the most valuable to all of us!

BATHING AND DRESSING

Everyday a disabled, chronically, or terminally ill child may need help to be toileted, bathed, and dressed. Depending on how much of this they can do for themselves determines the time and effort required by their parents or caretakers.

We found a supported toilet seat with side arms that fit over our toilet so Cam could be left with some privacy. A very ill child may need to use a bedside commode, pan, urinal, or diapers. When Cam got too heavy to lift in and out of the tub, we found a waterproof chair that stayed in the shower. We had to completely dress him, and found the hospital bed with the elevating back helpful. We also chose clothes that were loose fitting and easy to take on and off. When he became a teenager we tried to keep "style" in mind.

Dennis and I shared and took turns with all of these responsibilities. I'm convinced this prevented total "burn out" for both of us. For a couple of years we had an in-home student (respite) help with positioning and homework for one hour after school three days a week. This was very helpful, providing me with time to help the other children and start dinner.

MAINSTREAMING AND INCLUSION

At different stages in your child's illness, it may be in his or her best interest to spend part or all of the school day in the regular classroom. This has been called mainstreaming or inclusion. Cameron experienced many different classroom and school settings over the years. Some of his education was in "self-contained" classrooms, where he spent all of his time with other special needs children.

Our first attempt away from the full time self-contained setting, to a regular classroom with resource and aide help, was frightening. There were a lot of changes and new experiences. After some adjustments I saw many of the benefits and wrote the following article.

> Today I watched my son act in a school play. He was the only child that had special needs. He is in an electric wheelchair, or like in the play rides a chain-driven trike. He also has slurred speech and is difficult to understand. In the play he took the part of the shoemaker with a significant speaking part. In preparing for the play, he told me that it was decided that they would all learn their parts by memory. I had thought many times, yet never said, "He can never do this!" I asked him to show me his part in the play and was shocked when I realized he had already memorized it.

> I was proud watching him. He enjoyed performing and felt good about himself. Although there were moments when people couldn't understand everything he said, they knew the general part. Children and adults who watched the play wrote him letters telling him what a good job he did and how much they enjoyed watching it. It was a big boost for his self-esteem. This was only one of many things that he was able to do that year.

Although it was difficult to make the change after six years of mostly self-contained instruction, we saw some benefits. He knows that he is different from his regular classmates. The first few days there were a few tears from comments made on the playground about him. Yet with the help of his aide and teacher, the children learned all about him. He realized he learns at a slower rate and works at a slower pace. The class learned to understand this also and accept him for his strengths and limitations. They have made him feel welcome, loved, and accepted. The adjustment was made and soon every time we drove by the school he wanted to stop and peak in and talk about his new friends and activities.

He had a hard time feeding himself and I told him he did not have to eat in the cafeteria in front of others. After the first day or so of eating in the classroom with his aide he decided he felt comfortable eating with his peers in the cafeteria. I always made sure I sent finger foods and things that were not only easy to eat, but not messy.

He learned to work slowly on the typewriter and computer. He learned to dictate quickly to his aide, and it was wonderful for him to fully express himself.

He enjoyed both his experiences and time with the regular classroom, and with the self-contained children. He had some great friends that taught him he was not alone in his challenges.

Another mother shares how her daughter did with mainstreaming:

> When Abby was three she started "early childhood" through the public schools for a half a day, until she was six and started going to full day in a self-contained classroom. We put her in a regular kindergarten classroom for part of the day with other children. It was a little scary at first, but Abby's social skills sky-rocketed! She learned that some of her behavior problems were not appropriate and that the other children did not act that way, and they were very good role models for her. She was in the first grade musical play at the end of the year and did wonderful. When they told me that Abby was going to be in the play and that they were going to perform for the parents that morning I wondered what was going to happen. All the way to the school I thought to myself, will she really do what the other children will be doing? Will the people make fun of her? I was very nervous all the way there, but I had my Camcorder and was going to be proud of whatever she did. The program lasted about thirty minutes and much to my surprise Abby sat through the whole program. She didn't sing, but she was definitely a part of it. I tried to film it with tears running down my face. They were tears of happiness and just feeling so proud of my daughter. She not only did it once that day but she did it three times in one day, of course everyone was there that night to watch her perform for the PTA meeting.

In later years some disabled or chronically ill teens can receive vocational training. It is usually in a sheltered and supervised environment. Some may be well enough in their remissions (periods of wellness) to work outside the home. (See Chapter 9 for more education information.)

DISCIPLINE

It is often difficult to properly discipline a child with an illness or disability. Sometimes their understanding is limited and it may seem unkind to always be consistent and firm. However, an impaired or ill child needs realistic limits just as other children do.

> Discipline is not the process of shaping and molding children into what the family feels he should be (which in most cases is a carbon copy of them) but rather helping them to become uniquely what they are [6, p. 127].

Time out and rewards work well as discipline tools for most children. If not, often special education teachers have been trained in working with special discipline problems and could help you. Other times doctors may suggest medications or behavior therapy.

Because Cameron was so physically delayed I was pleased when he finally learned to reach out and touch things. It was difficult to say "no" when he would reach for my plants, spill the dirt, or turn the knobs on the T.V. and radio. It was also a delight to hear him finally fight back with his brothers. The first time he got angry and yelled, "You dummy!" We all understood his speech and were thrilled, even though we asked him to use kinder words in the future! We tried to reinforce the positive things, and explain those parts of his behavior that were not acceptable.

A BALANCE

Raising a disabled, chronically, or terminally ill child poses many situations that are difficult. There are only so many hours in a day and I seldom felt I had enough time to do all that was needed. This was confirmed when my four year old asked a friend on an outing what the round orange thing was he was peeling. He then turned and asked me why my child didn't know what an orange was. I had the startling realization that I didn't feel I had time to peel oranges, so I bought apples, bananas, etc., because they were faster to serve.

We worried as many parents do, and asked ourselves the same questions over and over . . .

> Were we giving him enough to eat? Did we stretch and work his muscles enough to prevent contractures or deformities? Was his education, therapy, and medical care all it could be? Should we mainstream him more or less? Were we giving enough time to our other children?

Each year Cameron became bigger and heavier. He was awkward to transfer and move about. He could feed himself, yet it was difficult, time consuming, and messy. There were days I would worry that he slept too much. I wondered if I should wake him to study or work on something (crazy!). I would think, "He has got to work twice as hard as the normal child to progress." This kind of compulsive thinking weighed on me, and was not healthy. Other days, I would find myself thinking the extreme opposite. I would tell myself, "Let him sleep, he can do little else, nothing will make a difference or change how he is!" With time and education I did find balance to my thinking.

RECREATION

Recreation is needed by all of us. It is important that you, your family, and when possible your ill child have some form of recreation. You may have to make many adaptions for this to happen. Some children are so ill that even a ride outside is impossible. You may have to bring recreation, games, music, or entertainment to your child. This may require creativity from a parent who is already exhausted. However, the results in behavior, attitudes, and well being for all of you, may be worth the work. Be creative, find ways to make the most of the time you now have together.

Cameron had an electric wheelchair. We tried to take him just about everywhere. It was a hassle getting his chair in and out of our van. It took time and muscle. However, he loved to watch his brothers play sports. He loved going to movies and eating out. (We helped him eat in public.) He loved to go camping and ride his wheelchair around the campground and trails. Because he loved going so much we tried making the effort to take him. Going places was one of the few things Cam and many ill or weak children are able to do.

Riding in a boat was another activity Cam could do well. He could sit up holding onto a rail inside the boat to stabilize himself. His hair blows in the warm wind as we whip through white-capped waves. The bumps are as much a thrill to him as a roller coaster to you or I. His squeals of delight can be heard above the roaring engine. His dad made sure he experienced water skiing by holding him on the skis. Cam's smile lets us know how proud he is.

He participated and enjoyed Special Olympics. In sixth and seventh grade he also took art and home economics classes. Although his aide did as much if not most of the fine motor activities, he still loved it and was proud of the finished products.

HOW MUCH SHOULD THE CHILD BE TOLD?

Many children are too young to understand their illness or different-ness. The severity of the illness does not always correlate with how well the child, or parents will cope. As parents we want to protect our child from pain and hurt. In my study of children dying from cancer, it seems even when parents chose not to tell their children they were dying, many seemed to have an inner sense, and would bring up their upcoming death to the astonishment of their parents. Honesty is an important principle for these children. Studies seem to confirm that often the children cope better with the news than their parents.

This seemed to be the case with us. Cameron seemed to accept his limitations often better than we did. In his own words he said writing to his schoolmates,

> You don't want to be handicapped, but I am still happy.

He then went on to tell what he wished he could do, still emphasizing those things he was able to do. We have always felt if our child is to live and function in a world with basically "normal" kids, they have a right to understand all they can about what makes them different. This can be done in a positive way over time. We tried very hard to do this while Cameron was still young. We planned on him living into adult-hood and we knew how teenagers can struggle with their self-image and self-esteem.

I fear for the child who is told they will learn to walk when they get older, and then never do. Or one who is told he/she will get better and doesn't. It seems safer for the young child to be told, "You may always struggle with walking, talking, or an illness, however you may improve." This approach may help them accept a wheelchair or com-munication board later as a teen. Or allow them to say their goodbyes before death. A positive, yet realistic approach may also help a child move forward while minimizing self-esteem problems and feelings of failure. Honesty and open communication seemed to comfort Cameron the most when his feelings were hurt.

SHOULD WE HAVE OTHER CHILDREN?

The decision to have more children can only be answered by you and your spouse, and the two of you may not agree. Know that you cannot replace a deceased child with another child.

Many of our friends did not have other children following the birth of their ill or disabled child. They were overwhelmed with the amount of work and care their child required. Many parents have additional fears that an illness or death could happen again. Unfortunately their innocence is gone, and they may now realize that bad things can and do happen to good people.

We chose to have other children. Each pregnancy was frightening. Of our seven pregnancies, we have four living children. While we were busy and often overwhelmed, we found many positive reasons for other siblings. Cameron faced a variety of experiences with his siblings. He was hugged and had his hair pulled at the same time by his one-year-old sister. One of his younger brothers would be playing with him one moment and telling him he was "messy and gross" the next. He got use to being confronted with an awful amount of honesty. Often he had his little sister on the back of his wheelchair or in his lap wanting a ride. Cameron only had a few friends his own age. This made me sad sometimes, however, I understood it was difficult for him to do the things they enjoyed doing. His siblings and caring adults provided most of his socialization.

Another fear parents have is that they cannot be good parents to additional children because they are so busy. Some have reported feeling guilty because they think they neglect their healthy children. One mother said,

> In our house you don't have a quick dinner and then run to the park. You have a long dinner while we feed Wilson, then we drive to the park, and by that time it's getting late and dark and we don't stay so long [8, p. 34].

Our children waited some too. They did their share of complaining, however, we felt it taught them patience, understanding, and selflessness. Children are resistant and can withstand more challenges than parents sometimes give them credit for. If we allow them to voice and accept their negative feelings, and then involve them in the problem solving, they can become a source of help. We met once a week as a family and discussed schedules, plans, and problems. We also tried to schedule numerous family trips and activities that kept us close. After twenty-four hours of traveling in a van to see grandparents, we all had a chance to demonstrate our best and worst characteristics! Fortunately we all enjoyed this time away and could always laugh about the struggles when the trip was over.

When Cameron was gone we all mourned and missed him terribly! However, having each other to love and support helped us through some of the loneliness.

SUGGESTIONS FOR FRIENDS AND RELATIVES

Parents of disabled, or terminally ill children can benefit from love, support, and help from friends and family. The old Indian saying, "Don't judge a man until you've walked in his moccasins," applies here also. Others may never fully understand how parents or these children feel. It may be hard to comprehend the depth of their emotional, mental, spiritual, and physical pain. One mother explained that one well-meaning relative told her not to think about the "fatal end" of her child's terminal illness, reasoning that we all could die at any moment anyway! This mom was frustrated and hurt because this relative couldn't understand the difference between her child's impending death and his own children who "might get hit by a car." Parents may learn to be patient with these kinds of comments. However, individuals who do respond with a listening ear, positive comments, or offers of help, can make a significant difference for these parents and their children. These parents face many responsibilities. Letting them share their fears and concerns is helpful. Parents often must decide when to discontinue medical interventions and offer "comfort only measures" when death is near. Sharing these and other burdens with others may lift some of the pain and concern from their shoulders.

Offering to relieve a parent for a short time can be a big help. Volunteering to learn and provide syringe or tube feedings, medicines, and breathing treatments. If they won't leave their child, offer to care for other children, run errands, do paperwork or even make calls to doctors, organizations, or insurance companies. The pressure of medical costs, filing claims, and asking organizations for funding is a significant emotional drain. Ask, "Where could I assist?" Or, "What could I do to help?" Or just volunteer for a particular job you feel comfortable doing. (I like the story about the man who showed up at the house the night before the funeral and polished all the families shoes.) Sincere efforts on your part often gives parents that little extra strength they need to carry on.

Some parents may seem to push their friends and relatives away. They want to handle everything alone. Understand this is a common reaction to stress and grief. Try to talk openly with them. Let them know you want to give them the space and privacy they need, however, you want to help them wherever possible. Don't give up, with time they may be able to accept your offers and reach out again to others.

OTHER'S FEARS

Feelings of pity, disgust, denial, and fear are all real feelings that people commonly experience when they first meet disabled, chronically, or terminally ill children. We can sometimes help by educating them about our child. This seems to aid them in developing better understanding and acceptance. It takes time and patience. I found being involved at school, in PTSA, parent advisory committees, and attending other meetings with teachers and therapists, increased everyone's awareness and understanding. I would ask teachers at school and church if I could come and talk to the class about Cameron's problems. I found that informing family and friends about Cameron's problems and needs helped them work through any uncomfortable or negative feelings they might have. Many of them, with time, became Cameron's dearest friends.

Unfortunately the disabled and chronically or terminally ill must on occasion face public rejection. Some people are offended that such a child, who eats sloppily, is brought to a restaurant. Some will not want to associate with the child for fear of getting ill themselves. This is extremely difficult on the child and parents. They all need love, acceptance, and friendship, now more than ever. Caregivers should strive to be discrete, yet unashamed in providing and promoting a social life for these children in spite of their differences.

FRIENDS FOR YOUR CHILD

Disabled, chronically, or terminally ill children desire friends just like healthy children. This is often difficult to achieve. If the child is too ill or weak to play and move as other children his age, it is often hard to convince the well child to become involved. It may require some creativity.

Cameron had a few good friends. Some had special needs and some did not. I would try and find fun things that they could both do together. Computer games worked the best because Cam did have one finger that he could use. Cam was particularly thrilled when one friend came over and put together a baseball card album for him. He basically just watched, but was thrilled with the end results! He was happy if someone would just talk, read, or even watch TV with him. Another friend seemed to see beyond Cam's physical body when he wrote the following poem for him:

> Cam the brave, so mighty and tall (Cam was short in physical stature for his age) you could beat anyone at all. (He was very weak.) Everyone knows you are cool, but only a few know you're mighty and tall! (Cam always wished he was tall like his brothers.)

Most of Cam's friends were caring adults that he learned to love. Our family appreciated their love, concern, friendship, and patience.

ACCEPTING YOUR NEW LIFE

Parenting a disabled, chronically, or terminally ill child will never be an easy task. We can choose chronic sadness and think our lives and dreams are shattered forever. Or we can pick up the pieces and incorporate this child into our lives and dreams. Yes, there will be struggles and anguish,

> There are a lot of problems, and many of them are huge. You think, "How can I get through this? But if you put all the disappointments on a scale and put all the joys on the other side, the joys would weigh a lot more [8, p. 16].

> . . . You don't believe you ever will recover at the beginning, but you get stronger, and you make it [8, p. 9].

> You'll find inner strength you didn't think existed. Pearl S. Buck in her book, *The Child That Never Grew,* said, "Be proud of your child, accept him as he is and do not heed the words and stares of those who do not know better. The child has a meaning for you and for all children. You will find a joy you cannot now suspect in fulfilling his life for and with him. Lift up your head and go your appointed way" [9, p. 59].

There were many times I didn't want to be strong and grow any more. I knew I was learning a lot of valuable lessons, yet it was hard work. My husband and I communicated our feelings and concerns and made plans together for our future. It seemed to help us find more peace and joy. Once we realized we were searching for a cure that wasn't there, we began to focus on what we could do with the new normal of our lives.

Once we let go of the child we wanted, it freed us up to give all that love to Peter [8, p. 7].

Parents can discover there can be joy in adversity, and find peace that can come from caring and serving an ill or dying child.

AN ATTITUDE OF GRATITUDE

Five negative Ds are Despair, Doom, Discouragement, Depression, and Denial. I wanted to keep these Ds out of my life. I knew if I allowed them to stay too long they would drive away my faith, hope, and happiness. I wanted to know how to look at the darkest cloud of adversity and carry on with a joyful heart. It was constant work to do this at first! I couldn't change my situation, yet I found I could change my perception and attitude about raising a child with problems. I tried hard to drive these negative feelings away. I tried to replace them by focusing on the positive things about my life. I had read about "gratitude therapy," . . . spending time each day thinking about those things you are grateful for in your life. In spite of all the hard work and worry, I did enjoy Cam's wonderful wit and humor. I had other loving children and many positive things to focus on and be grateful for. I didn't want to become bitter and angry at life and God. By focusing on the positive, I grew to realize my child's life was valuable, meaningful, and had purpose. I still feel I saw his limitations realistically, yet found joy in having him in our home. We were all much happier and enjoyed more fully our time together.

THE LOSS

Is anyone really ever prepared for their ill child to die? Even when you know it is nearing, and have experienced anticipatory grief and closure, the actual event may be overwhelming. How do you decide when it's time to pull away life-saving measures? How much medication do you offer to numb the pain, yet not over sedate? You may wonder, "Have I answered all my child's questions about death?" How can you hold on and let go at the same time?

Before your child becomes unconscious you may want to discuss the fears and questions as simply and honestly as possible. The not knowing is often worse than exact details.

Death is often near when your child begins to become confused and loses consciousness. This can happen slowly over many days. Your child's breathing and heart will become irregular as everything slows down. The skin color fades to a pale or grayish color. Hands and feet begin to get cool to the touch. Some children have seizures in the end.

There may not be anything worse than watching a child suffer. The memory may haunt you for a long time. There are medications that make it more comfortable. Be assured that in the end, dying is usually painless. Many who have "died" for a few minutes and are revived describe the event as sweet, peaceful, and pleasant.

We put our hearts, minds, and time into helping our child be the best he could. We were proud of every step he made. We loved and enjoyed him, yet it was hard work. As his mother I viewed caring for Cameron as a huge challenge. Now that he is gone after fourteen years, we have found the real challenge is trying to live without him. I miss his smile, his cheerful patient disposition. His presence filled our home, and now we deeply feel the void. Peace does come, yet it has required much time, patience, and work.

We felt his life on earth had purpose and value to us and all who knew him. He was happy with his life, wheelchair and all. He talked often of his "next life" and what he might find there. We find comfort in his hope, that he is free from his limitations and experiencing the "next life" that he often spoke of. It is with this same assurance that we are able to let him go.

REFERENCES

1. DSM-1V, *Diagnostic and Statistical Manual of Mental Disorders* (4th Edition), American Psychiatric Association, Washington, D.C., 1994.
2. S. R. Covey, *Principle-Centered Leadership*, Summit Books, New York, 1990-91.
3. F. Kupfer, *Before and After Zachariah*, Delacorte Press, New York, 1971.
4. M. L. Jones, *Home Care for the Chronically Ill or Disabled Child*, Harper & Row, New York, 1985.
5. N. Finny, *Handling the Young Cerebral Palsied Child at Home*, E. P. Dutton and Co., Inc., New York, 1975.

6. L. Buscaglia, *The Disabled and Their Parents: A Counseling Challenge,* Charles B. Slack, Inc., Thorofare, New Jersey, 1975.

7. C. Brown, *My Left Foot,* Simon and Schuster, Inc., New York, 1970.

8. R. Simons, *After The Tears,* Harcourt Brace Jovanovich, Orlando, Florida, 1985.

9. P. S. Buck, *The Child that Never Grew,* Woodbine House, Bethesda, Maryland, 1950.

CHAPTER 4

Building Self-Esteem and Self-Worth

What exactly is self-esteem and self-worth? What is the difference between them? How can we develop or build it in ourselves and our children? These were some of the questions we ask ourselves when we discovered we were the parents of a disabled child. It took fourteen years of learning, watching, and working hard to understand a model we feel can be helpful to anyone, including disabled, terminally ill children, and their siblings.

SELF-WORTH VERSUS SELF-ESTEEM

Clinical social worker, Fred Riley, has shared some important concepts of self-worth and self-esteem. We found helping our children understand the difference between self-worth and self-esteem can enhance their view of themselves and the world around them. It can also help parents understand the unique role and value of their chronically or terminally ill children.

Self-esteem is defined as: "WHAT I DO."

Self-esteem is often based on society's standard of what our behavior or performance should be. Self-esteem focuses on "doing" or having things. It is often controlled by the opinion of others, and the goal is often to impress others and thus feel good about ourselves.

Self-worth, on the other hand, is defined as: "WHO I AM."

Self-worth is focused on "BEING" rather than "DOING." It is gaining confidence, happiness, and peace—based on attitude and belief. It

49

does not require the opinion or evaluation of others. Self-worth comes from the inside out, rather than the outside in. Self-worth is based on who you are deep inside, how you view yourself and others. Self-worth requires understanding that your existence is not by chance. That you were created with a purpose. That you can grow and develop in spite of your limitations. Your goals and aspirations are character based. Self-esteem can also help you feel good about yourself. Abraham Lincoln said, "If you do good, you feel good." HOWEVER EVEN IF YOU CANNOT PERFORM IN ANY WAY YOU CAN STILL MAINTAIN YOUR CHARACTER AND SELF-WORTH. Stephen Covey in his book *Principle-Centered Leadership,* said:

> Internal security simply does not come externally [1, p. 84].

In the newsletter "Growing Together" is a discussion on how we over-schedule our children with activities and sports:

> . . . Parents need to help their children realize they are valued for who they are, not what they do [2].

This concept has been valuable to us, our family, and especially our disabled son.

Finding joy and happiness in Cameron's small accomplishments was difficult at first. It took time, work, and thought control to really feel the difference between "doing" and "being." I was always very task oriented. I was able to work hard, fast, and felt great when I thought I had accomplished many things by the end of a day. As a first born, I learned how to get recognition first by my parents from "doing" things. I received good grades and learned to play the piano and the violin. As I grew up I fed my self-esteem with church and community projects hoping to make the world a better place and help me look good. I also completed a college education and did some modeling and commercials which also helped me feel attractive, accepted, and important. It took time for me to understand that it had become an addiction. I needed to keep "doing" things to continue feeling good about myself. The reality for me and unfortunately for many others, is that one can rarely "do" enough "things" to satisfy the addiction. You may even damage your health and experience anxiety or depression trying! I finally learned that "being" was much more permanent than "doing"!

When Cameron was born, I began to discover that he would never do all the things I had done to build my self-esteem. I was his mother and felt responsible for his physical and emotional care and growth.

How would I accept this less than "normal" child? How could I help him accept himself in spite of his limitations?

My first reaction was to immerse myself into learning everything I could about his problems. I wanted to give Cameron every opportunity available. I wanted to say he was the best he could be. No one would or could say if he would ever walk, so we worked ("doing") long and hard assuming he would. It took me many years to accept he would not.

I soon learned it would be a very slow process and that small accomplishments would measure Cameron's success and progress. I remember how sad I felt when one doctor said Cameron would not be able to talk. So we helped teach him how to use a communication board. He learned to use it very fast, and then he surprised us all by saying some of the words. It wasn't long before his slurred speech was faster than using the board, and he could be understood by many at home, church, and school.

Cameron's first partial sentence was a small miracle and great thrill. He was three years old and this was the first day that he would go to a special pre-school without mom, all alone on a bus. As I was dressing him I could see the anxiety in his big brown eyes, those eyes always melted my heart. He looked up at me and uttered, "Mamma go?" Tears came to my eyes and I cheered, "You talked, you talked!" With great emotion I explained he would be going to school alone, but I would be home when he returned, and we were going to have some great communication together and make the most of his limitations! He had communicated and I had understood!

Other parents will have children who may never speak with words. These parents may need to look deeper for qualities in their children's personalities and spirit. Building from the inside, and focusing on self-worth, and the importance of their existence ("being") needs to be emphasized. Listen to the feelings of the mother of a non-verbal child as she expresses pride and unconditional love for her child.

> There is so much to say about raising a less than perfect child. We have been through the grieving process of not having the perfect child that we waited for. . . . The self-pity that sometimes I would drown myself in, and then the happiness that she brought to us, it felt like our emotions were on a roller coaster ride that never stopped. She has taught us so much. I feel very lucky that God chose to give us this special child. Raising a child that is different is very exhausting, but very rewarding and you learn to appreciate life more.

Cam's dad seemed to understand the concept of self-worth and "being" much easier than I. He would go once a week to the school and work with Cameron's physical therapist. He wrote,

I appreciated the beautiful grin that was always present on Cameron's face when I would walk into his classroom. One weeks visit had special significance. For weeks Dan, Cam's therapist, had prepared me for something very special. Cam was four or five years old and could only move himself by rolling on the floor. Today he was sitting on a little tricycle with his feet strapped to the pedals. He was in the middle of the school hallway. Slowly with great effort he started to move his trike toward me! The pleasure, excitement, and pride I felt is hard to describe. Though he had moved only a few inches in my direction it was the first time in his short life that he had demonstrated his ability to be upright and mobile. I realized at that moment that my pride in my son was no less than that of other fathers who had watched their children overcome great challenges and succeed. I knew Cameron would never be the star quarterback for a high school football team, or compete with his peers in other areas, yet at this moment, I felt joy and pride for a child who was doing his very best with the abilities and talents he possessed.

I had seen the same kind of strength and courage with another young teen, Brian Alexander, who was dying of cystic fibrosis. I remember vividly talking with him at his bedside as he prepared me for his ultimate and upcoming death and funeral. I remember his concern for others who had healthy bodies and would live long lives. His empathy and concern for them somehow seemed to be intensified rather than diminished by his struggles with life and his upcoming death. I often found myself contrasting the attitude and peace of mind that Brian and Cameron seemed to possess with others who struggle and have great difficulty finding personal peace and happiness.

I reflected on another young man, badly burned, who was on a psychiatric unit, who had difficulty finding a reason to go on with his life. I found myself contrasting the many limitations that Brian and Cameron had in comparison to the healthy physical body possessed by this young man who had attempted suicide on many occasions. I wondered why it is that many who seem to have a bounteous portion of life's greatest opportunities ultimately find themselves discouraged and distraught, feeling their lives are meaningless.

It was then that I began to more fully realize the benefits it can make in our lives when we understand the difference between self-esteem and self-worth. How fleeting self-esteem can be. I reflected on the lives of many who had acquired great financial, political, or career success, yet in the end chose to abruptly end their lives because they seem to lack a true inner sense of peace and worth. The things we do, our physical attributes, and the way we dress all have an impact on how we see ourselves on a daily basis and effect our fragile self-esteem. In contrast self-worth which comes from the inside out, and is based on who we are, can be permanent. Self-worth is personally controlled internally by those who possess it. Individuals possessing true self-worth are still effected by the loss of friends, possessions, physical health, appearances, etc. Nonetheless they seem able to find deep within themselves a worth and a value that carries them through those difficult times. Unfortunately much of today's values and society are built upon a self-esteem model that focuses on looks, performance, and obtaining possessions. Our attempt to dress and act in prescribed ways is all designed to increase our esteem and value in society's eyes. Sadly, since the ultimate appraisal of how we are doing comes from others, outside, rather than within, it can be very fleeting. Ultimately our physical talents and possessions will be left behind, and if we do not have internal insight and love of self and others we too may find ourselves lacking the strength to go on in the face of adversity.

UNCONDITIONAL LOVE AND ACCEPTANCE

We all want to feel confident and happy with "who" and "what" we are. This may seem like a challenge for the child who is so ill or disabled that they can do little more than exist. They, like many, may not be able to care for themselves alone. How do we as parents love and accept these children unconditionally? And possibly more difficult, how do we help them love and accept themselves? Harold Russell who lost both hands in combat stated,

> The only way I could feel at ease with them other people was if they felt at ease with me, and the only way for them to feel that way was for me to feel at ease with myself [3, p. 185].

We must realize that we cannot change the personalities of others. However, we can influence their positive behaviors and characteristics through unconditional love and acceptance. Unconditional or unmerited love builds self-worth.

Child development experts tell us that children are resilient. Even when we make mistakes, if we are truly trying to help our child with their best interest in mind our unconditional love will often overshadow our mistakes. Our children seemed more than willing to forgive us when we offered our apologies for our errors.

Experts tell us that children with

> low self-esteem perceive a discrepancy between who they are and who they would like to be [2, vol. 9-3].

At times parents may encourage their children to have too high expectations of themselves. In the newsletter, "Parents Make the Difference," the writer states,

> Unrealistic expectations can harm your child's self-esteem [4, vol. 4-4].

Our children seemed to benefit more if we would encourage them, while accepting their current performance . . . it is a fine balance.

Dennis remembers a large assembly of children in elementary school who were asked,

> If their parents told them that they were coloring outside the lines, and their picture was not pretty would they want to draw more? Of course the majority called out aloud, "No!"

When children consistently feel our acceptance and unconditional love, they experience an increase in their self-confidence.

Research indicates that when children feel self-confident they earn better grades, have more friends, and view their relationship with their parents more positively. We found building that relationship is vital in building a child's self-esteem. Parents sometimes don't realize that children are more likely to develop self-confidence when they establish positive relationships with their children through implementing clear rules and consistent discipline [2].

Self-love precedes our ability to love and accept others. We can try to avoid harsh judgments or be critical of the self. We all have a tendency to compare our worst with what we think we see in others . . . usually their best! Unfortunately children do this also, especially those who have visible physical differences, or who are in the grief cycle. We need to protect and build the self. It's okay to pamper and treat ourselves good. One way to increase our self-love is to understand the following principle:

God's love is unmerited and not predicated on our performance, or what we do. He loves us unconditionally.

When we feel and accept God's unconditional love for us, we feel more self-love and worth, then in turn we may help our children feel it too. Helping our children understand they are loved and valued unconditionally by God, parents, teachers, and hopefully by friends, may help them accept and cope with their situation and illness.

All children deserve to be loved and adored. Our children love to hear how much we wanted them, and how happy and thrilled we were when they arrived. This feeling of belonging builds self-worth. Helping our children focus on those things they can do, rather than those things they can't do, lifts their self-esteem as well as self-worth. A little saying I created that has helped me appreciate my children is,

"Don't expect . . . just accept," never limiting them from what they can become.

Again this does not mean there is no encouragement or discipline. In fact, children with low self-esteem often come from families where there is harsh or overly permissive forms of discipline. We feel a combination of clear, firm, and loving discipline balanced with reasonable age-appropriate freedom and independence lifts self-esteem and encourages the development of personal self-worth.

Accepting a child unconditionally is not always easy for parents. Often it means "letting go" of control and encouraging independence or self-reliance. Research has shown independence is the foundation of self-esteem, and that it may be damaged by attempts to over-control.

We tried to listen attentively to what our child said. Most children will benefit by verbalizing their feelings. Repressing or stuffing feelings is generally not healthy. Our feelings are usually there for a purpose. Telling a child they "shouldn't feel a certain way is generally not helpful. Allowing and accepting your child's feelings enhances understanding, self-esteem, and builds your relationship. Never stop talking to your children. Never give up. Continue offering honest praise and encouragement with lots of love, acceptance, and warmth.

IDENTITY

We begin to form a perception of ourselves at an early age. This identity includes personal characteristics, body image, abilities, and disabilities. Many of these perceptions are learned from experiences with our environment, and relationships with others. Leo Buscaglia in his book, *The Disabled and Their Parents,* says,

> One learns about and creates oneself during each moment of awareness. One is continually amalgamating his new learning with his old knowledge about himself and forever integrating it into an ever changing concept of self. Once basically formed, this concept of self extends outward from ourselves and becomes mostly responsible for our perceptions or impressions of the world and others [3, p. 183].

According to Christian psychotherapist, Dr. Les Carter, our behavior is determined in great measure by how we view ourselves. He said,

> It's safe to say that the self image is the core personality ingredient which directs every aspect of our being. The way we communicate, the way we handle our emotions, the way we behave publicly as well as privately is all a commentary on our image of ourselves . . . [5].

A positive self-concept is important for all of us. How we feel about ourselves influences how we respond to others and how we perceive they respond back. A poor self-image may set a negative pattern for a lifetime.

The disabled, chronically, or terminally ill child will develop similarly as other children. Yet they will often have special challenges that could contribute to a low self-esteem. I list some of these challenges as does Leo Buscaglia:

> 1. . . . negative, degrading, and devaluating experiences with interpersonal relationships. 2. Mental and physical discomfort and suffering . . . 3. Difficulties with social acceptance and rejection. 4. Limitation of experience, all which can lead to emotional suffering and inferiority feelings [3, pp. 184-185].

NEGATIVE LABELS

It took time for me to understand that we are in charge of our thoughts and feelings as well as our actions. Dennis had to remind me that, "No one can make us sad or angry, we choose to feel that way." I saw I had some bad habits when I read the book, *Eliminate Your Self-Defeating Behaviors,*

> Through our lives we tend to maintain many unnecessary and burdensome recurring thought and behavior patterns [6, p. 1].

We learned these patterns to help us cope with a particular situation in life, and continue with them long after the original situation changed or is gone all together. The author explains that one way we disown responsibility is to attach a negative label to ourselves. Our children do this also. If they tell themselves something long enough, it can be a self-fulfilling prophecy. ("For as he thinketh in his heart, so is he" [7, Proverb 23:7]). "I am ugly." "I am lazy." "I am dumb." "I can't learn." "No one likes me." All of these statements can damage us or our children's self-concept.

The disabled, chronically, or terminally ill child may respond with very similar negative labels, "I've tried it before." "I can't." "I'm afraid." "My friends will laugh." These self-defeating statements may limit a child's abilities as well as his self-image.

As parents we can first dispel, or avoid instilling these labels before we can replace them with new positive labels. Of course parents cannot shield a child from all negative situations. Peers, teachers, and siblings also try to affix negative labels to our children.

> Honest and open communication is the key to preventing self-defeating behaviors from developing and being maintained in our lives . . . [6, p. 161].

> Self-defeating behaviors based on faulty perceptions are kept alive and hidden within the individual when either good communication or sufficient love are missing. . . . In those stressful moments, people tend to say or do damaging things to children and let the damaging impressions stand unchallenged and unchanged in the child's mind [6, p. 162].

We tried to listen actively and effectively to our children. We tried to serve as models by using positive talk with ourselves as well as our children. Communication is difficult to implement if we are too busy or angry. This seems to be when thoughtless or damaging things are said. Mr. Chamberlain says,

> These negative concepts need to be talked out so that the child does not hold them as negative possessions that hinder individuality and limit or cripple potential [6, p. 162].

Putting our children first, when possible, helps them feel loved and important. It can give them the extra confidence they need to succeed at whatever level they can.

We tried to help Cameron love life in spite of his limitations. He made it easier because he seemed to generally have a cheerful disposition. I know this is not the case with all children. Often he seemed happier and more satisfied with life than our other "normal" children! He loved people and found satisfaction in small and simple things. We tried to feel and express our unconditional love to him often. We tried to help him realize he was different, yet to be proud of who he was and what he could do. We were proud he was our child, and tried to show it by taking him with us. We took him everywhere possible and tried to let him do whatever he could. We told him we enjoyed being with him. We actually meant it!

He was sensitive and tender and his feelings were hurt by insensitive remarks. Sometimes he would get mad or hurt by one of his brother's negative comments. He would seldom yell, hit, or try to get even. He seemed to express his hurt in kinder ways. These qualities were all part of his self-worth. He did not have the talents emphasized in TV commercials that promise sex appeal, popularity, or beauty. We tried to help him feel he was still a great human being the way he was.

I remember when a little boy asked if he could play with Cam's new Christmas truck and horse. Cam said, "Yes!," hoping the boy would play with Cameron too. The young boy said, "No, he didn't want to play with Cameron because he was ugly!" Cameron said, "I am not ugly!" (He really was a handsome young man.) He handled it very well. It was I who left the room crying! I didn't want Cam and the others to see my tears and know that my self-esteem wasn't as strong as his! He helped teach me the true meaning of self-worth and the value of each human being. I hope reading some of the following experiences and writings will help you see how he viewed life and how this view of himself helped him feel content with who and what he was.

LIFE REVIEW

At eight years old Cameron is still handsome despite the spastic muscles that exaggerated his smile and movements. He takes life pretty serious now. He wants to get good grades in school. Sometimes we would hear him talking to himself, as we drew closer we realized he was praying! He uses his slurred speech often, and now has access to a typewriter which really helps him communicate. Although he only uses one finger, he started writing stories and poems with wonderful themes. One of my favorites was about his chain-driven trike.

> My bike can fly! Oh my, oh my, oh my!
> My bike can fly,—in the sky so high, way up high.
> Do you want to try, do you want to try?
> My bike can fly, If not, you'd better take a hike,
> Unless you'd catch a ride on my bike.
> My bike can fly! Oh, my, oh my, oh my!
> My bike can fly in the sky so high!

He even starred as the "Shoemaker" on his trike in the school play, "The Elves and the Shoemaker."

He would tell you the highlight of his life was when he received an electric wheelchair as a gift from some very special people.

His first day out I watched him gliding up and down, ever so smooth he flowed along our steep driveway. He'd never been able to move like this before. He would go forward, backward, and in circles. The smile on his face told of his joy. He is alone, as he often was. But soon the neighborhood children surround him, admiring his new wheels. It's cold, so I call out to him. "No," he says, he is not cold! "No," he does not want to come inside! He can almost keep up with the other boys now. He is proud of his new "legs" and the attention he is receiving.

Now he will be able to get on and off the bus alone. He can travel at school from class to class and to the playground without waiting for help. The electric wheelchair increased his self-esteem and the increased interaction with peers helped him feel his self-worth.

He is small for his age. Very little muscle surrounds his limbs. Every bite of food or spoken word is an effort for him. He rides a bus over an hour to and from school. I know he gets tired, but he seldom complains. Simple things I do without even a thought require all of his energy. His teachers say he works and tries hard. They also comment on how cheerful, cooperative, and kind he is. He worries often how others are feeling. He usually remains courteous and patient as he waits for teachers (and me) to help him do the many things he cannot do for himself. When I get discouraged or depressed, I look to his example. I try harder to reach my own potential with more patience.

I tried to help him do everything he wanted which sometimes took more time, work, or energy than I had. One day he told me he wanted to be a boy scout like his oldest brother. I tried to drop the subject fearing it would be too hard for him. Could he memorize the scout oath and scout pledge? Would the scout leader be able to understand his slurred speech? He would ask me often to look at the cub scout book, he would read and try to understand what he would need to do to be a scout. He seemed so determined! "Okay," I said, "I will help you!"

He memorized the oath and pledge, and learned what was expected. The Scout Master told me he knew the material better than most of the boys and said, "Yes, he could become a cub scout!" It wasn't always easy for him, yet he loved it. He earned his wolf, bear, and a few arrow points. He received his arrow of light, Faith in God award, and got more than half of the merit badges toward his Eagle Scout award by his death.

At age ten he was writing creative stories slowly with one finger on the computer. Many of them displayed his humor and his innocent faith.

Why The Turtle Has A Shell

Many years ago before man was born, there lived a shell-less turtle, named Bowles. The sun never went down. Bowles' back kept getting sunburned because he doesn't have protection.

Bowles started out walking and looking for a shell. He comes to God and he says, "I want a shell to protect my back from the sun." God tell Bowles to go down to the orange tree. Bowles says, "What will I do down there? Those are new oranges. They are sour and green." Once again God tells Bowles to go down by the orange tree.

Slowly Bowles crawls toward the orange tree and sees a new path God has made for him. He crawls beneath the tree and a very large green orange hits him on the head. The orange breaks in half and the juice is like rubber cement. It is Bowles' new protection. He pulls his head into his new shell and goes to sleep. Sweet dreams!

THE TEEN YEARS

The teen years can be a difficult time for many children. As they grow from childhood to adulthood, many struggle to find who and what they are or want to become. The self-image seems much more vulnerable to one's physical appearance and performance. Self-esteem seems more fragile during this time. It may be more apparent to a disabled, chronically, or terminally ill child that he is different from his peers. Again experts have found that parents who keep communication open are better able to handle the challenges of adolescence.

Some teenagers in Madison, Wisconsin, listed some of the ways they'd like their parents to communicate, and our's agreed:

> Don't pressure us to achieve all the time. Praise us . . . sometimes it seems like nothing we do is good enough. Tell us you love us—even if we act like we don't want to hear it. Be honest . . . it makes us feel dumb if we were lied to. Don't yell! Let us form our own opinions . . . chances are they'll be a lot like yours. If we have a major problem, help us . . . don't solve it for us. Give us a chance to disagree . . . without telling us we're "talking back." We love to hear about when we were little. . . . Never stop talking to us." These same principles apply to our ill or disabled teens [4, pp. 4-6].

Many of these children may have the added stress of feeling different in their appearance. It may bring on intense insecurity when he first becomes aware of his differentness and body image. Peer pressure becomes more important at this time, however research shows that the family influence is generally a stronger factor. We can do a lot at home positively to combat this negative social pressure. We found self-worth principles and good communication are necessary.

Teenage depression and mood swings can occur with all children. Rebellion can occur with changes in their usual behaviors. The realization of an illness may have just occurred to them. It will take time to process these feelings and confused emotions. Some also tend to shut down communication lines. If they won't talk to you and you are concerned, try a teacher, school counselor, or seek professional help.

We tried to prepare Cameron for the teen years long before he arrived at that age through open communication. We tried to share with him some of the feelings he may encounter. He had watched his older brother struggle with similar feelings. We were surprised that puberty arrived as soon as it did! However, we were impressed how his internal self-worth carried him through some tough situations. We would like to share some more of his journal, writings, and feelings, to show how self-esteem and self-worth can develop in a disabled or terminally ill teenager.

VIEW OF SELF

By thirteen years old Cameron likes girls, and even has pimples to worry about. He has mastered controlling his electric wheelchair. He peddles a chain-driven tricycle in Special Olympics. He enjoys an art class and home economics. He makes lots of fun things with the help of his teachers and aide in sixth and seventh grades. He is pretty good on the computer and writes a short essay called:

"A Day in My Life" by Cameron Ashton

I wake up and it's Saturday. And usually I sleep in, somedays when it's cold I stay in. When dad gets up he dresses me. Then I watch T.V. till my breakfast is ready. After I eat breakfast I usually go to my brothers soccer games. I go in my van that has a wheelchair lift. After that I go shopping, or eat pizza, or go on a boat ride. I can swim with a special life jacket or ring. At night I watch T.V. or a movie, and eat pizza. (He loves pizza like most teens!) I have to stand in a special standing table that helps my hips. Then I go to bed in an electric (hospital) bed that's real cool. I sleep on my stomach, or side without a pillow. That's all folks!" (He developed a good sense of humor too.)

He also asks me to help him write about his problems to help his classmates understand him better. We constantly tried to help him understand and accept his disability.

Cerebral palsy is usually caused from lack of oxygen to the brain. It happens most often at or before birth. I had a hard time being born. It took a long time. My heart almost stopped so the cells in the motor center of my brain died. So now my brain can't tell my body to move properly. The cells that help me hear, see, and think were not damaged. Some kids with cerebral palsy have many more problems than me. Just the motor center of my brain were damaged so I can't move like you, or even make my mouth move properly to talk clear like you do. Sometimes it's hard to do my work because my hands are slow, or my aides can't understand me. You don't want to be handicapped, but I am still happy. (He was able to focus on the positive things.)

He chose to be involved in church and school activities. He was thrilled when he was nominated to the National Junior Honor Society the week he turned fourteen.

I remember one summer day we had all been water skiing and it was too cold for Cameron to swim or ride in the large water tube. His dad sensing maybe Cameron felt left out said, "You know Cameron I couldn't ski as well if I didn't have you watching and cheering me on. I try harder because you motivate me to really reach out for all six buoys in the competition ski course." Tears started to fill Cam's eyes. I don't think he knew until that moment what a support and impact he had been to his father's life. This seemed to boost Cameron's self-worth and let him know how much we liked having him along. He attended several water ski tournaments and even cheered his dad and older brother to victory a couple of times.

His self-esteem was lifted when he went to special camps and the Special Olympics program. The children competed in their wheelchairs and bikes. He enjoyed meeting and playing with other friends like himself.

A copy of a school personality interview gives us some idea of how he viewed himself.

"What would you never change about yourself?" "My name." "What is the most important thing you own?" "My electric wheelchair." "What is your greatest achievement?" "To learn to read." "What is your favorite toy?" "My computer." "What are you like on the inside?" "Happy!" "What do you want to be when you grow up." "A mailman, bus driver, or teacher, and a big tall man!" (He was short for his age, the rest of the family is tall.) "When are you the happiest?" "When I go out of state and visit my grandma (and grandpa)." "When are you the saddest?" "When I have to leave." "If your life ended today what would you like people to say about you?" "Hey, that was a neat kid! He also had a cool wheelchair." "Who do you love and admire most?" "God, and my mom and dad."

A year before his death he expressed some desire for freedom in the following writing:

I want to travel in space, where no one would find me. I will then build a city on the moon. (I will put cable TV in!) I will build moon cars and there will be no laws! (Doesn't that sound like a regular teenager's dream?!)

Six weeks before Cam's death, his father was asked to speak to a local college class on caring for a child like Cam. His dad decided to make a video to show the class what Cameron was really like. It seemed helpful for the class to see how he spoke, moved, and responded. This is most of what he said that spring day. It took well over an hour to tape it. His speech was slow and labored. The video depicts Cam's view of himself in many areas.

> Hi! My name is Cameron Ashton. It not easy being different. (He was realistic.) It look easy, but not really. It like hard, I guess. Like for example, I can't do a lot. But I can play with my computer, and I hope to learn more about the computer so I can teach my mom and dad to use it and stuff. (He looks for the positive.) I hope you understand me okay, and can learn what it like to be me. (He was concerned for others.) It's fun to ride my bike, and wheelchair, it's like walking for me. I can swim with a little help from this (holds up some arm floats.) (His focus is on the things he can do.) I have a trampoline, it over there, (pointing) and I can jump on it, I mean I can lay on it and have somebody jump with me. (He's honest.) My family is really nice. My dad helps me get dressed in the morning and helps me go bathroom and all that. I have aide who helps me work good at school. (He feels appreciation to others.) Here my suggestions to you college helpers. Be nice to handicapped kids because it hurt their feelings. (Sensitivity) I really feel that I can walk in the next life, and that I can talk better. (His faith and hope.) And that I live forever in the next life after this and that I will see God again. (His belief in a God and a next life.) And I get to see my Grandma and Grandpa who died a couple years ago, again. And you can too someday. I guess I don't have to say anymore. And this is Cameron signing off. (His humor!)

We feel his inner self-worth and greatest strength came because he believed in God and believed he was a child of God. When he was just two years old he wanted to pray. Some of his first words were, "I love God," as he would gaze upward. Somehow Cameron grasped these principles as a source of strength and comfort.

In the Bible (John 1:12), it states that Christ gave "us power to become the sons of God" [7]. If we could empower our children with this principle it may give them something to live for in spite of their difficulties. It may help them feel their true self-worth, value, and purpose, realizing they are a son or daughter of God. Acts 17:28,29 . . . "We are the offspring of God" . . . Romans 8: . . . "We are the children of God" [7].

We will never forget what Cameron has taught us. We know there is great joy and peace in "being," and also value in improving talents and focusing on what we can "do." However, our life has purpose, and meaning no matter how short or how limited. Self-worth comes from deep inside us and is not limited to what we're able to do. Cameron helped us recognize that all human life has meaning. We are all children of God with self-worth and value in spite of how limited our abilities may be.

GONE TOO SOON

With puberty and it's growth spurt we began to see an increase in many of Cam's physical problems. His scoliosis (curvature of the spine) was harder to control by the brace he had worn since age eight. His hips had started to dislocate in spite of his standing table and physical therapy (which is common with cerebral palsy). After my own research, I agreed with the doctor's suggestion, that hip surgery was the best solution. It should eliminate Cameron's pain and additional deterioration of his hips and spine. The surgeon also hoped for improved standing and transferring skills.

Cameron was excited to get out of school a week early in May. His teachers had let him take his tests early and he had received his usual high grades and finished everything that was expected of him. He had always enjoyed his visits to the hospital for check-ups, and x-rays. It was a wonderful children's orthopedic hospital, one of the best in the country.

He sat behind me as I drove our van thirty minutes to the hospital. I could feel his anticipation. He was nervous and excited all at once. We visited x-ray, lab, anesthesia, and had doctor's exams. He was very brave. While we waited I kept busy with personal paperwork. Cam read magazines and had me read from a book a neighbor had given him. It felt good just being with him. I always felt busy at home with five children, and often felt guilty because I could never do everything I felt needed to be done. But now I was just relaxed, basking in the warmth of his pleasant personality and enjoying our one-on-one time together.

It was fun to see his face light up when we were all finished and they brought him one of his favorite meals for lunch . . . a hamburger and fries! I left him in his hospital bed with a game and a movie to go home and feed my other children. His dad got off work about an hour later and came to spend the night. The two of them had fun together. They watched movies and ate more fun hospital food. They even played "James Bond" and escaped from the floor in his wheelchair for an unauthorized tour of the hospital! Later his dad got him all showered for surgery which was scheduled early the next morning. He then slept next to Cameron in a fold-out chair bed. I talked to them by phone that night, and again before he went into surgery. I was glad we had made it a habit to tell each other, "I love you."

He handled the five-hour surgery well. We greeted him in recovery as he moaned with pain. I stayed with him during the day and his dad spent the evenings and nights at his side. He was pretty restless that first night and depended on pain and muscle relaxing medications.

The next day I enjoyed giving him his bath and helping the nurses with his care. He was in a close observation room with one other patient. They felt he was well enough to be moved to a regular room, but one was not available. He remained under close nursing care for another evening.

That night I kissed Cam good-bye and teasingly told my husband to take good care of him and not to let him "code" (die). I went to bed at midnight. Soon after I had fallen asleep, the phone rang and I received the terrible news.

Cameron's ICU nurse had just taken his temperature, pulse, respirations, and blood pressure about 12:00 midnight. They were all normal, in fact his tachycardia (fast heart beat) had slowed down some. She had measured his urine output and asked him if he hurt. He said, "No." She told him, "That if he wanted to sleep on his stomach that was all right for a while longer. He said, "OK." She patted him on the shoulder and said, "I'm glad you feel better." He had not needed pain or muscle relaxing medication for a while.

His dad was grateful an hour earlier he had been by his side when he made his final request to be turned over (as we had done so many times over the past 14 years). At about 12:30 A.M. the nurse was returning to her desk after being with the other child in the room; she looked over at Cameron and thought he looked too "still" and came over to his bed. His dad woke up as she called a "code" and others came rushing to resuscitate Cameron's now lifeless body. It was never determined why his heart stopped so suddenly and they could never get it going again. I arrived at the hospital soon after. We then had to face our greatest challenge and began a painful walk that would become our longest journey through grief.

REFERENCES

1. S. R. Covey, *Principle-Centered Leadership,* Summit Books, New York, 1990-91.
2. Dunn and Hargett Inc., *Growing Together Newsletter,* Lafayette, Indiana, 1993.
3. L. Buscaglia, *The Disabled and Their Parents: A Counseling Challenge,* Charles B. Slack, Inc., Thorofare, New Jersey, 1975.

4. The Parent Institute, *Parents Make a Difference Newsletter,* Fairfax Station, Virginia, 1993.
5. Minirth-Meier Media Ministries, Richardson, Texas, 1994.
6. J. M. Chamberlain, *Eliminate Your SDB's (Self-Defeating Behaviors),* BYU Press, Provo, Utah, 1978.
7. Authorized King James version, BIBLE, A. J. Holman Co., Philadelphia.

CHAPTER 5

Recognizing and Managing Our Grief

When Cameron died we were intensely overcome with the deepest feelings of pain, distress, and sorrow, we had ever experienced. Yes, we had experienced loss and grief before. Our reactions and the duration of grief were different with each situation. We had studied grief and helped others. However, we had never actually FELT its impact so deeply. We were lost and helpless. We realized to manage our grief this time, we would need additional knowledge and support to help us deal with the magnitude of this loss *on* our lives. We hope that sharing what we learned on our painful path will help you. We hope the tools we've found will maximize your journey toward growth and recovery as it has ours.

Many situations can bring grief to us. In fact approximately one in four people are experiencing grief at any given moment [1]. Many are not prepared and don't understand what they are feeling. Most of us did not study loss in high school or college. Professionals often use loss scales to judge the potential impact of various losses in our lives. For example, in the DSM-III-R a child moving out on his/her own is listed as a MILD stressor, loss of a job is rated MODERATE, divorce is listed as an EXTREME loss, death of a spouse as SEVERE, and death of a child as CATASTROPHIC [2, p. 11]. These are then rated with other factors, including personality traits, to formulate a diagnosis and treatment plan.

Society seems to esteem those of us who appear emotionally strong, so many of us hide or repress our feelings. Often this adds to our distress and we aren't able to accomplish our grief work. It takes courage to take the necessary steps to reconcile our grief. Yet, it is with that courage we may begin to recover and live again.

In the beginning we found we weren't able to choose or control what we were feeling. Later on, we had more control and could choose or decide how we would grieve. We could go through the "motions," and often the appropriate "emotion" would follow. We also noticed an accumulative effect, especially if there wasn't sufficient time to recover between events. Remember, grief can be experienced in a variety of ways depending on our former experiences, circumstances, philosophy of life, and the nature of our loss. Most of us are affected by grief in the following areas: Intellectually, Spiritually, Physically, Socially and Emotionally. We will address the stages, processes, dimensions, and some of the more common symptoms of grief (see Figure 1).

INTELLECTUALLY

It may take significant time and thought for your mind to really understand or accept what has happened to you. Your brain will have to adjust cognitively to this new information. It will take time for the disbelief and shock to soften so you can mentally process what has happened.

We have found that if parents intellectually understand some of the grief process and theory it can help them accept their painful emotional feelings. The knowledge of what they are experiencing seems to help them understand their feelings are normal, and that they are not going "crazy."

Some may also try to intellectualize the details of their loss without allowing feelings or emotions. When they are ready to do their "grief work" they may need help to transfer this knowledge from their heads to their hearts so they can feel their emotions. "Feeling is healing."

SPIRITUALLY

Your spirituality is a unique dimension of your religion. It could be defined as your relationship with God and how you feel you fit into the universe. Religion is how you nourish your spirituality. Many individuals will rely on their spiritual strength or religious beliefs to get them through life's challenges. While religion and spiritual feelings can and do bring a great deal of comfort, we have found it helpful to also utilize and apply knowledge of the grief process. There are many

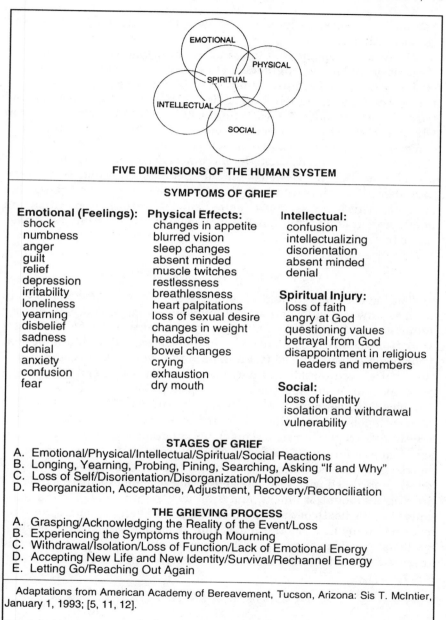

FIVE DIMENSIONS OF THE HUMAN SYSTEM

SYMPTOMS OF GRIEF

Emotional (Feelings):
shock
numbness
anger
guilt
relief
depression
irritability
loneliness
yearning
disbelief
sadness
denial
anxiety
confusion
fear

Physical Effects:
changes in appetite
blurred vision
sleep changes
absent minded
muscle twitches
restlessness
breathlessness
heart palpitations
loss of sexual desire
changes in weight
headaches
bowel changes
crying
exhaustion
dry mouth

Intellectual:
confusion
intellectualizing
disorientation
absent minded
denial

Spiritual Injury:
loss of faith
angry at God
questioning values
betrayal from God
disappointment in religious
    leaders and members

Social:
loss of identity
isolation and withdrawal
vulnerability

STAGES OF GRIEF
A. Emotional/Physical/Intellectual/Spiritual/Social Reactions
B. Longing, Yearning, Probing, Pining, Searching, Asking "If and Why"
C. Loss of Self/Disorientation/Disorganization/Hopeless
D. Reorganization, Acceptance, Adjustment, Recovery/Reconciliation

THE GRIEVING PROCESS
A. Grasping/Acknowledging the Reality of the Event/Loss
B. Experiencing the Symptoms through Mourning
C. Withdrawal/Isolation/Loss of Function/Lack of Emotional Energy
D. Accepting New Life and New Identity/Survival/Rechannel Energy
E. Letting Go/Reaching Out Again

Adaptations from American Academy of Bereavement, Tucson, Arizona: Sis T. McIntier, January 1, 1993; [5, 11, 12].

Figure 1. Common symptoms of grief.

healing principles, including faith, which can help us achieve full reconciliation.

Many people for the first time in their lives turn to God and faith in their crisis and are strengthened. Others are confused and angry with God, clergy, or their church family. At first many cannot feel spiritual feelings and question their faith. This spiritual injury is a common and normal grief response. We will offer explanations and helping ideas in Chapter 8. With time and work, it seems most of the spiritually injured can return to their faith and beliefs for comfort.

Ronald Knapp in his book, *Beyond Endurance,* reported that most of the parents he interviewed believed their child existed somewhere after death. They believed and had great hope for some kind of next life [3, p. 35]. This belief seemed to help them deal with the separation and death of their child. This spiritual hope may be what ultimately brings peace to many people.

PHYSICALLY AND EMOTIONALLY

The list of acute symptoms is endless (see Figure 1). You may feel an intense physical pain and aching anywhere and everywhere as your numbness wears off. You may experience a tightness or hollowness in your stomach or chest. You may feel breathless, a dry mouth, or that your heart is pounding so fast and hard that you feel you could surely die, or wish you would! You may be restless, unable to sit still, or feel so weak and exhausted you cannot possibly move. Many experience changes in bowel, appetite, and sleeping patterns. You may feel irritable with noise or any stimulation. It may be difficult to concentrate on anything except the loss. This preoccupation can lead to absentmindedness for an extended period of time. You may experience headaches, blurred vision, or nervous twitches. The immune system is often suppressed with grief. Research has revealed mourners have an increased amount of illness, and even death, up to two or more years following the death of their loved one [4, p. 5]. Their physical symptoms may be intensified by other emotional reactions, which could include guilt, depression, anger, anxiety, resentment or bitterness. We will discuss some of these emotions individually.

SHOCK, NUMBNESS, DISBELIEF, AND DENIAL

How can this be? This is not what you wanted or expected! It confirms all you've heard and feared, yet never felt so deeply, "life is not fair!" "Why us?" You may feel numb or in a state of confusion and abandonment. The disbelief, sadness, loneliness, fear, regret, and despair may overpower you. It may be difficult to feel happiness, joy, love, or spiritual feelings for a long time. It may be hard to concentrate on even simple tasks. Your normal coping behaviors may be exaggerated. Grief is unique to each individual. No one will feel the pain exactly the way you do. Grief is immeasurable, difficult to describe, and impossible to comprehend. Our expression of grief is often a display of our love. The depth of the love, time, service, and EMOTIONAL INVESTMENT coincides with the depth and duration of our grief. Grief work is some of the hardest work you will ever do. It takes lots of time and patience. It requires effort and energy physically, emotionally, spiritually, and intellectually.

When Cameron died, I didn't know the human eye could produce so many tears. I cried everyday for three months, sometimes several times a day. I was concerned like many, that crying so much wasn't healthy. However, I learned when I would allow myself to feel the pain and let the tears come, I could let go of my emotions for a while and somehow function better. I didn't understand until later that repressing our feelings is usually not helpful.

> Tears shed during grief have more toxins that do regular tears.
> Tears actually can be healing [5, p. 8].

With all of our losses, Dennis did not cry as often or as much as I. We grieved in different ways and we will discuss the differences in men and women's grief in Chapter 7. For me, as for many others, crying was a healthy way to start my healing process. The shock and disbelief would come and go. It took a long time to believe this could really happen to us. Like many other parents, we certainly wished it hadn't!

For some, denial may remain for weeks, months, or even years. Sometimes friends and relatives contribute to this denial. They may think or say something like "I won't talk about it if you don't" [6]. We found discussing our pain was good therapy. Some may go a step beyond denial in their attempt to cope. This is called repression: an unconscious forgetting of the traumatic event. You aren't even aware you're not thinking about a painful emotion. You stuff it far from your conscious memory. Unfortunately, emotions usually must be dealt with on a conscious level or they may appear as a physical illness, generalized anxiety, panic attacks, post-traumatic stress syndrome, etc. It can be a long, hard road.

It is normal not to disturb a loved one's room or possessions for a while. We chose to move most of Cameron's equipment soon after his death because our three-year-old daughter shared his room. She was ready to move out of her crib and have a "regular" looking girls room with pink furnishings.

There are many other needed changes and adjustments that at first we may deny. Be patient, with time, denial can subside and eventually most will be able to let go of those things that are not needed. It is generally recommended and healthy to save some keepsakes that bring comfort and special memories.

HURT, CONFUSION, AND ANGER

Your friends, relatives, and co-workers may be uncomfortable around you. They may seem to ignore you because of their awkwardness. They may not understand the intensity and duration of your grief or may feel helpless to console and comfort you. Consequently, many offer cliches or platitudes as a source of comfort. You may hear some of the following:

> Your child is better off now, the suffering is over. Get over it, put it behind you. You're lucky it did not last any longer, time will heal. There in a better place, God needed or wanted them. They won't need a wheelchair, treatments, or medicine anymore! Your other children can use your time now. Be strong, don't cry. You were lucky to have them as long as you did.

Although some of these statements may be true, they often felt like attempts to negate our grief, as if others were telling us not to grieve. These statements hurt, yet there is little we could say, or do, to answer these statements offered by people who sincerely wanted to help. Because they have not had our experience, it is difficult for them to understand the depth, and length of our grief.

This lack of understanding I felt from others was very difficult for me. I wanted to tell them how much I hurt and how they didn't understand. After reading the following poem I realized there was no way others could feel or understand my pain, they meant well and I chose to be patient and simply say, "Thank you" to their efforts.

WHAT DO YOU SAY

What do you say when a baby dies and someone says . . . "At least you didn't bring it home." What do you say when a baby is stillborn and someone says . . . "At least it never lived." What do you say when a mother of three says . . . "Think of all the time you'll have." What do you say when so many say . . . "You can always have another . . . At least you never knew it . . . You have your whole life ahead of you . . . You have an angel in heaven." What do you do when someone says . . . nothing? What do you say when someone says . . . "I'm sorry." You say, with grateful tears and warm embrace, "Thank You!" [5, p. 72].

Anger may hide many other feelings. Anger repressed or consciously turned inward often leads to guilt, confusion, and depression. Actually, anger can be a sign of healing, so don't stuff it. It often means your experiencing unmet expectations or needs. You may feel angry at doctors, nurses, or God for all the suffering your child experienced. For a time you may feel life is meaningless. You might feel angry at God for allowing your child to suffer and be ill, only to die in the end (see Figure 2). To deal with these intense feelings of anger try using these four A's.

"Admit" your feelings, don't keep them buried deep inside. "Analyze" your anger, where is the real anger coming from (medical people, clergy, friends, or family)? "Act" on your anger through talking, writing/journaling, weeping, or following up on an issue. Sometimes writing a letter to whom the anger is directed is helpful, even if you choose not to mail it! Realize you do have choices as to how to "act, not react." (Thinking is too passive.) "Abandon" or "Accept" your anger, ultimately letting it go by forgiving yourself and others [1].

"Accept, don't expect" often helps us let go of unrealistic expectations or attempts to control others. We then may reduce our frustration level and avoid some of the side effects of unresolved emotions and issues.

GUILT

"Guilt feelings are often a combination of many different feelings rather than one simple feeling. . . . It's a messy mixture of insecurity, self-doubt, self-condemnation, self-judgment, anxiety, and fear" [7].

Guilt might be the most painful component of grief for parents. Most parents have been taught or feel strongly that they are responsible for their children's well-being. Most parents provide care and love their children with great emotion and effort. When a child becomes ill, dies,

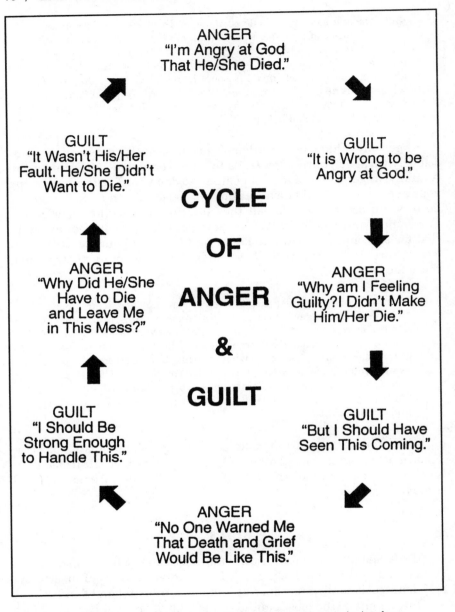

Figure 2. Cycle of anger and guilt. Reprinted with permission from the American Academy of Bereavement, Tucson, Arizona. Author: Sister Teresa McIntier. Copyright, January 1, 1993.

or commits suicide, parents may ask themselves over and over, "How could they have prevented this from happening?" "What did they do wrong?" "How can they undo this terrible event?" The guilt words, "I should have," or "shouldn't have" may haunt parents for a long time. It is an overwhelming burden for parents to carry and endure.

Guilt was a strong emotion in the death of Cam. The following is what I wrote about guilt soon after the loss of Cameron.

I was surprised by our doctor's advice. He informed me that Cameron's hips had deteriorated and he would need to do surgery within six months. Our appointment that day was for his scoliosis (crooked spine) and for his back brace adjustments. The doctor had simply ordered the hip x-rays as a second thought.

A few years earlier in another state, doctors had told us he might someday need hip surgery, but that he was doing so well it could be years away. So I had almost quit asking and worrying about his hips.

I could see tears swelling up in Cameron's big brown eyes, I had always bribed him into standing in his prone standing table, and working hard at his stretching exercises to keep his muscles from getting tight and his hips from dislocating—all to avoid the "knife of the surgeon."

I tried to reassure Cameron. I said, "During the surgery he would be asleep and it wouldn't hurt. Also that when he woke up he would get medication to keep him comfortable." I told him all the benefits of the surgery. The doctor had thought maybe his knee pain was coming from his partial hip dislocation. The surgery could possibly remove this pain so he could ride his adapted trike better. I reminded him of his two good friends that had similar successful surgeries. One was now able to walk some with her walker. Cam was so trusting and obedient. He would do whatever we felt was best for him.

Because I was a concerned mother and pediatric nurse, I wanted to know every detail and names of all the procedures. I went home and researched everything out, getting other professional's opinions. After a lot of time and study I agreed with the doctors, Cam would have the surgery. We planned it when school would be ending, six months away.

Dennis and Cameron trusted the doctor's and especially my decision that surgery was best. I am reminded of the movie, *Robin Hood* with Kevin Costner. Robin had made what he thought was the best decision in behalf of his beloved and trusted blind friend, Duncan. He sent him away from the fighting and danger . . . only to find that he had been ruthlessly murdered anyway! Robin Hood felt enormous sorrow and guilt! Duncan was so perfect and obedient, Robin didn't feel he deserved to die. The guilt he felt for his decision was apparent. Then his partner, The Great Azeem, seeing Robin's anguish replied, "There are no perfect men, just perfect intentions." Most parents also have "perfect intentions" for the child they love. Sometimes beyond their control, something goes wrong. Even with the best plans, accidents happen, children become ill or die.

As the parents of a disabled child, we both felt intensely responsible for his safety. He had always trusted and depended on us to care for and protect him. My intentions for Cam's health were perfect. However, my decision ultimately cost him his life! This guilt weighed heavily on me. I asked myself many questions over and over again. "Where had I gone wrong?" "Why hadn't God warned me?" "Why had I encouraged the doctor to do all the procedures at once?" "Was it more than Cameron could handle?" "Why hadn't I, the pediatric nurse, spent the night?" "Could I have prevented his death?" It took a long time for me to understand that these kinds of feelings and questions were normal and common. With time, work, and faith I was finally able to resolve my guilt.

Dennis felt intense guilt also. He was the one lying next to Cam when he died. He had kissed him good night shortly before and was relieved he was resting so well with less pain. Had Cameron tried to call out to him? Should he have noticed something was wrong?" Had Cameron aspirated or choked as one nurse and doctor thought, while his father slept next to him? Why didn't he hear something? The nurse was always in the room, why hadn't he asked her to watch or listen closer? How could he ever let go of this painful blame and guilt? He sincerely felt he had let me and Cameron down by falling asleep. He cried uncontrollably for hours after. Neither the children, nor I could comfort him. He and Cam had showered, dressed, brushed teeth, and often shared the same fork for fourteen years. The void and guilt he felt were beyond measure. He was a family counselor and had helped others through their grief, yet felt lost at first and unable to help himself.

We had both presented grief workshops and had experienced guilt before. We now realized we may have intellectually understood guilt, however we hadn't emotionally felt or carried the intensity of this pain before. We had no idea that guilt could hurt so much and for so long.

We learned there are no clear cut answers for everyone on how to relieve guilt. We have found that in many instances people are feeling "False Guilt" (blaming oneself for events and circumstances you are not really responsible for). False Guilt can be resolved over time by hearing and expressing healthy and accurate thought processes and then by integrating them cognitively. The four As can be applied to guilt and many other emotions you are struggling with. Remember, ADMIT the feelings, don't stuff them. ANALYZE where the guilt is coming from, is it a true or false guilt. Remember False Guilt occurs when we feel responsible for something that is out of your control. ACT on your guilt through talking, writing, crying, or getting more information. ABANDON these feelings by forgiving yourself, understanding that God loves you unconditionally. You might try eliminating "shoulds" from your vocabulary. (If someone else shames you with too many shoulds, you could respond back with, "Don't SHOULD on me!") In fact you may "wish" you had done something different. It is normal to feel that way. These feelings need to be expressed. Unresolved guilt is not healthy. If you did make a true mistake, Dr. Thurman reminds us "To Err is Human." None of us are perfect and we all make mistakes. You must let go and forgive yourself [8, p. 23].

DEPRESSION AND HOPELESSNESS

Depression is usually an illness that involves mood, thoughts, and behavior. Depression usually accompanies grief, and is a normal feeling after a loss. When events seem beyond our control, the helplessness we feel often leads to depression. Some of the symptoms may be sleeping too little or too much, eating too little or too much, loss of energy and drive, inability to function at home, school, work, or sexually. You may feel tired, weak or ill, and not want to dress or bathe yourself. You may often be worried, overwhelmed, and anxious. Anxiety often leads to depression. You may feel agitated and tense over what you have to do next, often without the ability to concentrate or even remember what you were going to do. You may feel empty, tearful, helpless, hopeless, worthless, and abandoned. You may move slow and feel dead inside. (Depression can be anger turned inward.)

Everyone has experienced depressive moods at times in their life. If depression persists it can become clinical, which may mean you'll need help recovering. My hope was not to get clinically depressed to the point of needing medication or hospitalization. I was willing to get the help if I needed it, I just wanted to use all my self-help tools first.

I had been taught for years by my counselor husband "to put a limit on my worries." I tried to do this with my grief. I knew "feeling was healing" so I did not repress my sadness. At the same time I would not allow myself to think only of my grief all day. I took time to feel, cry, etc., and later I found positive (cognitive) thought control helped me cope. I would try to control the amount of time spent in my grief-work. If it wasn't a good time or place to cry, be sad, or have a negative thought, I would try to think, "stop" and try to replace the sad emotion with another more positive thought or action.

It is also important that you get enough food, rest, and exercise. This made a big difference for my husband and me. Especially vigorous exercise that can raise your endorphins and help give you a feeling of well-being. Research has also shown that sunlight to the iris (eyes) can increase serotonin levels in the brain like antidepressants do (call SAD# 301-496-0500 for artificial light information). A brisk walk outside provides the benefit of light and exercise, and also allows some meditation time! We found reading, writing, praying, and meditating can lift depression and bring some comfort. Don't take on too many tasks or expect to function normally for awhile. Don't make major decisions for approximately a year after a major loss whenever possible.

It is important to do the things that normally bring you happiness and pleasure. For some this may be to order pizza, go to a movie, or buy something special. We tried to do the fun things we enjoyed doing before Cam's death. Nothing felt as enjoyable at first, yet with time, work, and patience we slowly saw progress.

Often when people need support the most, they drive friends and family from them because they are so depressed. This may cause the mourner to feel more guilt and depression. They wonder why they aren't better. They may get angry because no one allows them to grieve. Some stuff all these emotions inside and end up clinically depressed. This is when professional help may be needed.

ANXIETY, STRESS, AND CONTROL

I responded to my loss with over activity, doing lots of tasks. I thought since Cam was gone, I could do EVERYTHING! I soon found myself anxious, stressed, and overly controlling. I had taken on more than I could handle. I found everything can seem stressful during grief.

Even the basics are difficult to manage in the beginning stages of grief. Often you feel out of control and powerless. This may bring about a need to over control people and events in your life that you have concern and responsibility for.

Whenever we feel stressful feelings we can ask ourselves, "Am I trying to control someone or something that is really outside of my control?" or "Is someone trying to over control me?"

If our child is disabled, ill, or has died beyond our control, we feel vulnerable and afraid. We then are more likely to attempt to over control others or our environment. We may find ourselves frustrated and angry when those around us won't do what we desire. It may cause us to feel hurt, rejected, and unloved. The more we try to control others, especially our children and spouses, the more they may pull away from us. If we can be patient with ourselves, love unconditionally, and "let go" of our need to control, we will eventually feel more peace and freedom.

I learned this principle as a teenager, although my application was somewhat immature and naive it helped me learn to let go of things outside of my control. As young girls, my best friend and I would walk in the hills behind our homes when we were frustrated with life. We would talk and try to figure out life's meanings. When we couldn't find explanations or felt we couldn't do anything about a particular situation, we would start trying to find something good about it, or put it in "God's hands." We coined a little phrase, "It's probably for the best." We have since learned that not all things outside our control seem to turn out good or even for the best, yet this positive mental attitude and "letting go" of the need to control has brought us increased mental health, and faith as adults. It is expressed well in one of my father's and grandfather's favorite poems by Reinhold Niebuhr,

> God grant me the grace to accept with serenity the things that cannot be changed. The courage to change the things which should be changed. And the wisdom to distinguish the one from the other [9].

Accepting and turning those things I could not change over to a higher source, truly "letting go," brought a great sense of relief to me. I had heard my husband say to our children many times, "It's usually not the situation that causes our stress, but how we view it. I've spent many years reframing how I choose to look at things. Viewing challenges as an opportunity for learning helps you avoid becoming a helpless victim of your situation. Try asking "What lesson can we learn from this." This attitude can add strength and fortitude to your coping abilities.

We may find it helpful to change our "Whys?" to "Whats" [1]. We may not ever understand "why" our child died or is ill, but we can learn what happened, and what to do now. This is a more appropriate form of self-control (see Chapter 8 for more "whys" and meaning.)

After the death of Cameron, Dennis and I found dealing with everyday stress more difficult. Even though we had lost a child we were surprised to have less tolerance for our other children. Our patience with everyone including ourselves was limited.

Again we discovered the benefits of physical exercise. It seemed to help reduce irritability caused by our stress. We found it was fun to exercise together. It enhanced our physical, mental, and emotional well-being, and contributed to a healthy marriage.

We learned how to say, "No," and to stop and think before saying, "Yes" and over-committing ourselves.

We found and utilized the healing power of touch and affection. (Touch and affection can be used with music as a relaxation technique.) Affection seemed to help our children also decrease stress while increasing their security and imprinting any lost identity. We will discuss additional help for family and children in Chapter 7.

I used to believe that rushing and doing two or more things at once would help me finish my tasks faster and give me an edge on stress. I learned in most instances this technique was not helping me. We are cautioned that trying to think of or do more than one thing at a time causes your mind to race and creates more stress [10]. Enjoy the moment you are in, taste your food, feel the shower water, or texture of the towel on your skin. If you are trying to meditate, don't allow your mind to race and wander. Observe your mind for clues to repressed feelings, or try to control where it takes you through concentration or visualization. I have tried to concentrate on the word "peace" over and over again when I am stressed at night and trying to fall asleep [10].

We tried different types of meditation and relaxation techniques during our grief. One that we like, involves either sitting or lying down, taking several deep slow breaths through your nose, exhale out your mouth moving your stomach or diaphragm. Then try to tense, tighten, or contract all of your muscles from head to toe. Hold them tight while you count to ten, then relax. Breathe again and relax. Do this a couple of times and picture yourself sinking deeper and deeper into your chair or bed, until you are totally relaxed. Some people do this with meditation and "inner child" work [10, p. 70] once or twice daily for ten to thirty minutes [10, p. 76]. Some claim that this dimming of the sympathetic nervous system relaxes them better than taking an anti-anxiety drug [10].

When you are stressed at work, or short on time, try the following quick stress management technique. Count to ten, take a deep breath, leave your situation, and take a short walk.

We also decided to be more faithful about weekly dates together. We tried to give ourselves permission to grieve. Spending peaceful time alone together helped us communicate and do our grief work. In time we knew we could also give ourselves permission to slowly "let go" of our grief, thus helping our stress and anxiety. We would never let go of the memories, just the lost future and dreams.

LONGING, YEARNING, PINING, AND SEARCHING

For us, this stage of our grief lasted the longest. We missed our son so deeply. This earth life seemed like a long time to wait to see, talk, or embrace him again. We wondered, as so many do, "Why us?" We kept wishing he was still with us. We tried to resolve questions that seemed at first to have no satisfying answers. I feel the following poem by a friend whose eight year old died describes this long, searching, confusing state:

Everytime I look at your picture I see a smiling, happy face
telling me, "I love you mommy" and hugging me at my waist.
Tears stream down my face as I think how much I miss you
and still see you each day in all the tasks I do as I go on my way

Everytime I see the Nintendo I imagine in my mind
You lying on the floor with sister rubbing you on the head
and crawling all over you as you smiled and played ahead
But all I really see is the Nintendo sitting atop a blank TV

Everytime I look out the sliding glass door I see you sitting on your
bike, or swaying on the rope swing or swimming in the pool
But all I really see is your bike sitting empty and the swing set
alone

Everytime I set the table I set places for the whole family,
There are six of us, aren't there?
But then I remember now there are only five and I remove one plate.

Everytime we get ready to go to school or anyplace I want to call
you
to help me, to load the kids or carry a bag, but then I remember
that my "Big helper" is no more,
and I walk holding everything sadly out the door.

Everytime I turn around I find something that reminds me of you
A coat hanging in the closet, or a ball sitting in the yard
A picture on the piano or even a simple shoe
This house is somewhat haunting because of the memories here
Sometimes I can embrace them, but then I remember they are only
memories and will never be real again.

Everytime I look at your picture I see a smiling face saying,
"I love you Mommy" hugging me at my waist.
Tears stream down my face
As I think how much I miss you and still see you each day
in all the tasks I do as I go on my way.

Parents who lose an infant through miscarriage, stillbirth, neo-natal death, or adoptive placement often struggle with "empty arms" [5, p. 7]. Some parents report, "Their arms ache." RTS Bereavement Services, an international perinatal bereavement program, emphasizes the difficulty parents have when they have to say "good-bye" without first really saying "hello" [5, p. 65].

Those of you who cared for your terminally ill child may feel intensely sad as you watched your child suffer beyond your control. Depending on your circumstances and its duration, you had to balance an enormous amount of time, energy, and decision making. You may look for support and often find their isn't enough to help you until the dreaded last days come. When death does come, does it bring relief, shock, disbelief, or confused ambivalence? You are often left baffled and uncertain as to what you have just experienced.

Parents may continue to yearn for their child's well-being or return for a long time. They yearn for the way things were and for what can never be. They search for answers, looking for hope or peace to return into their lives again. They continue to ask, "Why?" They start to wonder if they will ever feel any better. They reason that they must be going crazy or doing something wrong to still be in so much pain. These feelings can be very confusing and may last for a long time. The fear of something else "going wrong" hangs over them. Life just doesn't feel right. This is the time anger, anxiety, and depression can set in. Everyone thinks you are better, and you hate to admit you're not. Parents find it hard to believe that it may take eighteen to twenty-four months to find relief, and additional years to functioning recovery. Never returning exactly to what life use to be, yet finding a "new normal" [5, p. 10], where peace and happiness can be felt again.

BARGAINING, WISHES, AND OVERACTIVITY

Bargaining during chronic or terminal illness, or after a death may be common [11, p. 82]. Parents and children may make promises to themselves, others, or God. In return they seek acceptance, improved health, or some other wish. This bargaining and wishing can go off and on for many years.

Trying to find reason and meaning behind a child's death or diagnosis is one of the greatest struggles parents will face. It will take time and healthy thought processes before you discover your own meaning and reconciliation.

As part of my grief work I dove into over-activity. It seemed to be an attempt to validate my worth and redefine my purpose. I used my busyness and doing tasks in an attempt to find relief and a feeling of acceptance through my accomplishments. Through my over-activity and bargaining I was determined to make my life significant, meaningful, and productive in the absence of my "special" child. I had lost some of my self-esteem and had to prove I was still useful and valuable without caring for a chronically ill child.

I chose to believe that others expected me to move on with a stiff upper lip. I tried to do this in a variety of ways. I volunteered to watch a pair of newborn twins, one named after Cam. I tried to support my children more in all their school, church, and sports activities. I redecorated Cameron's room for my three-year-old daughter, and made drapes for other rooms. I went back to work on the Pediatric Unit a few days a month. (My hospital work was a constant reminder that my child didn't recover like most do.) I planned many family camp-outs and trips. (This was difficult because Cameron enjoyed traveling so much.) My husband and I planted new trees, shrubs, and flowers, making a memorial for Cam. We joined a fitness club and tried doing many other new things.

I've learned it's part of grief to try to find happiness by over-doing or over-buying. All of this over-activity helped me cope as best I could. However, at first nothing seemed to make me feel better.

If one stays in this "over-active" or "under-active" mode for long periods of time they may become stuck in the grief process and not totally resolve their feelings. Feeling is healing and we need to find the time and make the effort to do our grief work.

LOSS OF SELF–DISORIENTATION– DISORGANIZATION

Any traumatic event can cause disorientation and disorganization in our lives. Serious challenges from our childhood or adulthood trauma may cause a suppression or loss of the true self. Abuse and other destructive experiences may cause a person to feel unaccepted with who they are. They then turn to pleasing behaviors which they hope will secure them the love and attention they need. Many professionals call these "masks" because they are not part of the true self [10, p. 57]. These people appear successful, yet inside many are confused, lonely, anxious, or depressed. An identity crisis may lead to this loss of self. Professionals may help individuals better understand the source of their insecurities through "inner child work" [10, p. 70]. This kind of therapy helps a person remember, reclaim, and confront those past pains that have been hidden away. Again, feeling the hurt and pain is often a way to heal. Many are able to relive or claim past behaviors, qualities or feelings in a safe environment with a competent professional. Those who repress or suppress grief may experience a similar loss of self. They try to hurry and be through with their pain and pretend to carry on as usual. Society confirms their behavior by telling them how strong they are, or how much faith they must have to recover so quickly. We then continue this false self to save face and look strong to others.

With the loss of any child you lose a huge part of yourself. Yet when a child has been totally dependent on you because of illness, or a disability, the loss can feel larger than life itself! It can complicate your grieving. You have given so much, for so long, that part of your self-image and self-esteem may be lost. This void can be enormous and adds unique dimensions to your grief. This is especially true at the death of a child who has received most of your time, thought, and worry for months or years.

I wondered what will I do with my time? How can I find my new self? As I tried to regain or redefine my identity, the void and disorientation felt more than I could endure at times.

WITHDRAWAL, ISOLATION, AND LONELINESS

It is common when we feel no one can understand, care, or respond to our pain for us to withdraw from our community, church, friends, and family. This is a normal grief reaction. It becomes unhealthy if this isolation becomes a permanent solution for our grief.

Often we isolate ourselves to the point of no return. We stop reaching out to others and sharing our concerns and feelings. Soon we find no one calls or comes, which may feel safer for awhile. Yet, with time, many become lonely and bitter and are unable to fully recover. They lose their ability to feel joy, interact with, or help others.

Ultimate loneliness may occur when we feel separated not only from other's understanding and love, but from God's. Watching your child's suffering through illness may haunt you for a long time. Why did they have to endure so much pain or suffer so long? You may also feel an enormous amount of guilt because you felt some relief when it was over. There are two songs written by Deanna Edwards found on the audio tape, *Learning to Live With Grief.* The first is called, "Teach Me To Die." The words are beautiful, as if sung by the terminally ill, "Many things I don't understand. Don't be afraid to say good-bye, then I'll teach you to live." The second song is sung to the deceased called, "We Will Walk in the World For You" [6].

HELP WITH THE FUNERAL

The functions and purposes of funerals are as important as other public rituals in our society. When we are born, married, or go through major changes in our lives, these rituals help us adjust and make the needed transition. Many times a funeral just happens. Especially if it was an unexpected death. The family may not have time to fully comprehend how aspects of a funeral can offer comfort and closure. Some have suffered remorse by decisions they were pushed to make when they were unable to think clearly, or they simply followed the advice of others. There are many decisions to make. Depending upon their beliefs or religion, do loved ones want a funeral, memorial service, wake, shiva, mass, viewing, or grave-side service? Do they want only family to attend? Where do we bury, or is cremation an option? An open or closed casket? What should we or the deceased wear? Who should speak, and what should be said? Music, flowers, location, casket, and headstone; so many things to think about when you are numb from shock, or in so much pain you wish you were the one who died.

Remember that it is generally helpful for families to participate as much as possible in the funeral and burial plans. It is also healthy for other friends and associates to come and acknowledge the death. They need an opportunity to express their emotions, love, support, respect, and feel closure by saying their good-byes.

I remember Dennis carrying our infant daughter's casket to her grave and offering a dedication prayer at the grave-side service. He told me, "This is the only thing I'll be able to do for my daughter." He also spoke at his mother's funeral after her suicide. He wanted to use some of her favorite music. (Not everyone would be comfortable participating so much.) The "counselor" in him wanted others to understand how someone could be so ill and hurt so deeply that they chose suicide. He was able to share the circumstances leading to her death, and also convey his and other family members' love for her, in spite of her challenges. All of my father's children spoke at his funeral. It was a wonderful tribute paid by those who loved him.

Not everyone wants to actively participate. I have seen letters written by family members and read at the funeral. This may help many who find it difficult to express themselves verbally at such an emotional time.

When Cameron died it seemed our world fell apart. Every decision seemed overwhelming. Because we had buried other family members, some things were already planned and understood. We knew we wanted him buried back home where his sister was buried. (We felt some peace when the funeral director told us they could move our infant's casket and headstone up to our son's location. In fact they put her small casket right on top of his!) We both wanted his favorite songs played at the funeral. We wanted a few of his words and poems read, and we even showed a short video of him. Dennis was determined to speak, I wasn't sure I could. I ended up reading a letter I had written to him the night he died. It was the first step in my grief work.

> Dearest Cameron,
> What a joy you have been in my life these last fourteen years. I have loved taking care of your physical body, and watching your spirit grow into such a fine young man. I've always been proud to call you my son. We have talked often of your limitations and what freedom death could offer. I had so hoped you could stay much longer!
> You loved Christ . . . your testimony and faith were so strong and pure. You've touched many people. I will miss you Cam, there will be such a void without you here, but I will have faith and wait until that glorious resurrection day when I will see you again, your body "whole," those beautiful brown eyes, your shining smile, sparkling personality, and strong, valiant spirit.
> All my love to you forever,
> Mom

We were exhausted after the funeral, yet received peace from the verbal expressions and love we felt. At first I didn't want to have two funerals. I just wanted to fly Cameron's body home to where his sister was buried and have a family funeral there. I am now very glad I listened to Dennis who felt we needed to offer closure to family and friends who had come to know and love him in our present home. We held the funeral on a Saturday and the whole school must have been there! There was standing room only for many. Before the funeral we stood by the open casket and many came and offered words of love and comfort. It helped us understand the function, purpose, and value of funerals and viewings more clearly.

Family and friends can bring you comfort in a variety of ways at the funeral. Don't be afraid to ask them to attend or participate. The following is some of what my sister said as one of the funeral speakers. We felt comfort and love from her comments. We were impressed at how others could carry a portion of our burden and pain.

> In the early morning before I had been told of Cameron's passing I awoke early and was unable to go back to sleep. I was filed with thoughts about Cameron. (He had his surgery 2 days before.) A sweet feeling of love for him filled me and I began to reflect on different situations I had with him. I felt some sadness as I remembered a moment when I had come to stay with him after his younger brother was born. I remember Cameron, age two years, wanting to go ride a bike with the other kids. My sister set him outside on the bike, but at that time he couldn't pedal, and how sad I felt. Then I reflected on the great joy we all had when he was able to ride a bike by having his feet strapped to the pedals. I remember him on their boat and when a water skier would fall Cameron would lift a red warning flag and smile with glee. As all these thoughts flew through my mind I felt such a great love and respect for his parents. For the care and love they had given Cameron through the years. I was so filled with this love for Cameron and his parents I got up and wrote Cameron a letter. I sealed it and set it on the night stand. Two hours later they called to tell us of Cameron's passing. I wish Cam could read the letter or at least feel of my love. This experience has been a source of comfort to me.

In her letter to him she shares how much he blessed her and her family's life. That he was a "light" on a hill to them. These kinds of experiences were shared by many in cards, words, and deeds. I feel this is how a funeral can bring you a peace that will last long after everyone has returned to their own lives, and you are left to try and remake yours.

After the funeral I felt some relief from the shock, numbness, denial, and guilt. As time passed I then went into other normal phases of grief. I will always be amazed at the intensity and duration of grief. The anger, anxiety, searching, emptiness, and depression came and went for a long time. Research findings indicate that most recovery for a major loss occurs in two to five years. Unfortunately, some will suffer profound grief much longer.

> Grief cannot be compared, measured, or quantified. . . . Healing . . .
> does not mean a quick cure; healing is putting the loss in perspec-
> tive [5, p. xiv].

Figure 1 reviews some of the symptoms, stages, and dimensions you may experience with grief. With time, work, and faith, our understanding gradually allowed us to move toward new horizons of joy and hope.

REFERENCES

1. M. Dickson, *Grief Recovery Seminars,* Dallas, Texas, 1991.
2. DSM-III, *Diagnostic and Statistical Manual of Mental Disorders* (3rd Edition), American Psychiatric Association, Washington, D.C., 1987.
3. R. L. Knapp, *Beyond Endurance,* Schocken Books, New York, 1986.
4. E. N. Jackson, *Understanding Grief,* Abingdon Press, Nashville, Tennessee, 1946.
5. R. K. Limbo and S. R. Wheeler, *When a Baby Dies: A Handbook for Healing and Helping,* La Crosse Lutheran Hospital/Gundersen Clinic, Ltd., 1986.
6. D. Edwards, audio tape, *Learning to Live With Grief,* Covenant Recordings, Inc., Salt Lake City, Utah, 1989.
7. B. Bush, *Guilt—A Tool for Christian Growth,* Catholic Update and Care Notes, Abbey Press, St. Meinrad, Indiana, 1991.
8. C. Thurman, *These Truths We Must Believe,* Thomas Nelson, Nashville, Tennessee, 1991.
9. R. Niebuhr, Public Domain, over 100 years old.
10. J. Borysenko, *Minding the Body, Mending the Mind,* Addison-Wesley Publishing Co., Inc., Reading, Massachusetts, 1987.
11. E. Kubler-Ross, *On Death and Dying,* Macmillan Publishing Co., Inc., New York, 1969.
12. J. W. Worden, *Grief Counseling and Grief Therapy: A Handbook for the Mental Health Practitioner,* Springer, New York, 1982.

CHAPTER 6

Reconciliation of Our Loss: Adjusting, Accepting, and Healing

> Everyone can master a grief—but he who has it!
>
> Shakespeare

How do we know if we are accomplishing our grief work and heading toward healing? How can we reorganize our life without our loved one? How do we accept death and find peace?

We eventually realized we wouldn't actually "get over" our loss. We would never be the same people again. This loss would become part of us, and part of our life's experience.

> ... grief becomes your "companion, and teacher" as you learn to live with it [1, p. vii].

If we do not face our grief it may not change or improve. We may want to avoid or repress our feelings to avoid the pain. However, this choice may increase our healing time. Most professionals agree that we must acknowledge our pain through feeling it in order to accept it. Mourning is an important part of our grief work. This doesn't mean there aren't times when you try to concentrate on other things. I like the analogy that grief is like a little child. There are times I could "hold" my grief, and other times I could send it out to play. If your child falls down and skins a knee, he/she comes inside crying for comfort. As caretakers we don't ignore the cry; we hold and comfort, put on a bandage, and then when he/she feels better we send him/her back out to play. We can do the same with our grief: there will be times we have to hold it, really feel the hurt, and then gradually over time, we can send it away [1, p. 37].

However, "holding our grief" or emotions for long periods of time without "letting go" (grudges and intense anger) can deplete serotonin levels in the brain and increase our chances for depression and delayed recovery.

Dennis and I took time to feel and communicate our deep emotions, without stuffing or repressing them. We then gradually focused more on letting go.

As you face your grief you may begin to get your life back into control. Facing your grief means taking an active part. It may begin as you help to plan the funeral, pick out the casket, select flowers, select a burial location, and headstone. Literature generally recommends that it is helpful for us to see, touch, or hold our loved ones before burial. You may want to ask someone to take pictures and save them until you are ready to view them. This visual evidence often helps our minds acknowledge and accept that the event really occurred. Often we are in shock and may not be able to remember important details we later wish to know or remember.

We would give anything now to have pictures of our first infant daughter and her little casket. We made sure we got lots of pictures of Cameron, before and after his death.

With time it is actually up to you to decide what your healing will or won't be. Recovery becomes an individual choice. Healing is a constant decision and requires participation. When we become so focused on ourselves and want everyone around us to meet our needs we may experience a longer healing time. Some people choose not to get well. Many choose this position because they may like the attention they get from family and friends. Some become dependent on therapy or medications and don't want to heal. Some are afraid to heal, they are frightened by their feelings. Remember recognizing and expressing feelings can be healing. It may be long hard work.

I found grief work to be the hardest work I have ever done. However, like most people, I wanted to "recover" and was willing to try anything to feel better.

Fortunately with work, time, and patience, the guilt, anger, and sadness consumed less of our time. We gradually became more comfortable with ourselves, our future, and our grief.

I was surprised at one intense experience occurring about eighteen months after Cam's death. I felt I had truly admitted and understood my loss until I ran into a friend of Cameron's named Laura. She was his age, height, weight, coloring, and had the same disability.

In fact, to me, she looked like she could be Cam's twin! When I saw her I wanted to run and hug and kiss her. I restrained myself, knowing this would scare her to death! I invited her mother to stop by the house with Laura, sometime soon. She came a few days later and we had a wonderful visit. We had bought Laura a little gift for Christmas.

After she left I cried and cried. She reminded me so much of Cameron. I had a full-blown "grief attack"! The deep painful emotions came flooding back and I was sad for several days. I didn't understand all my feelings. I started thinking, "Should I adopt a disabled child or find a nursing job where I could be near disabled children." As I discussed my confusion with my sister later, I explained, "I didn't really want to feed Laura, dress her, put her on the toilet, or lift her heavy chair. I just wanted to hold, talk to, and be near her." My sister then helped me realize I probably didn't miss the hard work of caring for Cameron (his disability), I just missed him! And of course I couldn't replace him by adoption, or a nursing job being near other disabled children. This experience helped me more fully understand and actualize my grief and loss. I learned these feelings are a normal part of grieving, and it wasn't long before seeing her or being around her was easier and joyful.

The most important concept for me to learn was that resolve and healing are relative terms. We "walk through" the grief cycle and can recover. Psalms 23:3 "I walk through the valley of the shadow of death" [2]. We don't have to get stuck down in the valley. Yet, it's best not to run out, or get a quick fix, or "get it over with" as so many try to do. Although grief doesn't ever completely leave, you can walk out a new person and learn how to live with your loss, and feel true joy again.

I even learned different ways to answer the dreaded question, "How many children do you have?" My response varies now depending on the person asking and the situation. With some individuals I felt I could share greater details. In casual conversation I discovered it was not necessary to acknowledge my losses.

We found that positive self-talk, and thought control also helped. We tried to focus on and feel grateful for the good things we still had in our lives (gratitude therapy). We knew regrets could be damaging if dwelt on. We found it was healthy to laugh, play, and take time from work and life's pressures. We found this difficult initially to do for an extended time. Joy and happiness are meaningful emotions that are dimmed by loss. We knew this lack of joy was a normal part of the grief process and so we tried not to put high expectations on each other. With work and time we found that the pain softened, and we could carry our sadness, rather than our sadness carrying us.

I will never be the same again, but I have reinvested new energy back into life. I guess I have gained some new insights and traits. I am doing things I have not done before.

What doesn't destroy me, strengthens me [3].

I have tried not to let my grief drive me from my faith or the good things in life. I hope I have grown in some ways, and become a stronger person. Yet I, like most parents, would rather have my child back than my character strengthened or improved!

HOLIDAYS AND SPECIAL OCCASIONS

There will be many painful memories that are associated with special occasions. Birthdays and holidays may be covered with an unspoken sadness that someone is missing. This shadow grief may begin days before the event. Grief attacks are common and normal. Some find it easier to break tradition and try something new. Change can be good and may make special occasions less painful. The first year is often the most difficult, so don't be afraid to let others know of your limitations. Try not to take on too many projects. Reevaluate why you do what you do and ask yourself if it is really necessary this year. If you must do certain things, decide who could help you? Try to graciously accept when others offer to help you.

Remember to eat a nutritionally balanced diet with plenty of fluids and avoid junk foods. Avoiding caffeine, tobacco, and alcohol will enhance physical and emotional healing through self-control. It is wise to get a balance of rest, exercise, and work. Reading and journaling can bring comfort. Writing down your thoughts or memories may bring peace into your heart during difficult days. Forgiving and service also may help.

We have observed over the years that those who were able to reach out to others, healed more rapidly themselves. Dennis noticed this when he worked in the psychiatric unit at the hospital. Those discharged the quickest were helping other patients. It may help them to forget their own pain for awhile as they focus on someone else. We tried to apply this principle to our own lives.

We remember one particular time when we found helping others did lessen our own pain. On our son's second death anniversary, which was near his birthday, we were feeling extra sad. We decided to celebrate his birthday by doing something special for someone. Dennis chose to help some people at church, and I took a meal to a woman who was home-bound. That night we found our own emptiness and loneliness had lifted.

Grief attacks may come and go for the rest of your life, especially on these special days. However, each year the pain may soften some as you learn to accept and live without your child.

The following is part of a Christmas letter one family sent out eight and a half months after the death of their eighteen-month-old daughter:

> The events of the years dictate that our usual annual attempt at yuletide wit be set aside, at least for a year, and give way to more serious reflection. For we approach this Christmas season with a new perspective born of pain and the healing and solace that comes thereafter. On April 10th of this year, as most of you are aware, we lost our precious daughter Michelle in a household accident. Our lives are forever changed.
>
> In the hours and days after that horrible night, you sustained us. Our family and friends surrounded us, physically, emotionally, and spiritually. You took us in your arms, held our trembling hands, let us soak your shoulders with our tears.
>
> Where the miles separated us, you sent cards, turned our home into a botanical garden, sent your prayers to the heavens on our behalf. You sacrificed time, energy, your means, and your comfort. You vicariously experienced the death of your own loved ones. You allowed yourselves to weep, to take our pain upon yourselves, to ease our burden, to search your own souls for answers.
>
> Some of you loved us or knew us well before this incident. Some were casual acquaintances. Others were veritable strangers. You represent many faiths, races, economic circumstances, and ethnic origins. But for one brief moment in time, our little Michelle made us one. One faith, one hope, one human family.
>
> I have since, standing at the grave of my daughter, often marveled at the power of a tiny life. A life so short, so seemingly nondescript by the world's standards. Had she lived, how much more could she have done to enrich and uplift others' lives? And in the final analysis, what else that we do in this life matters?
>
> Regardless of our faith or creed, Christmas universally represents a celebration of sacrifice. The life of Jesus Christ was devoted to sacrifice. It culminated in the ultimate sacrifice. Your sacrifices on behalf of our family over the last eight months have been worthy of

His example. You have been our saviors.

While our faith provides so much guidance, WE DON'T YET HAVE ALL THE ANSWERS TO THE PROFOUND QUESTIONS RAISED BY MICHELLE'S PASSING. OUR GRIEVING WILL LAST OUR LIFETIMES. BUT TIME AND PRAYER TAKE THE EDGE OFF THE PAIN. AGONY RIPENS INTO LONGING. DESPAIR TURNS TO SOLACE. THIS CHRISTMAS SEASON IS ONE OF MIXED EMOTIONS FOR US. THERE IS EMPTINESS OVER THE MISSING STOCKING ON THE WALL. BUT THERE IS A RENEWED APPRECIATION FOR THE ATONEMENT OF JESUS CHRIST. THERE IS ONE LESS SET OF LITTLE HANDS TO ADORN THE TREE. BUT THERE IS A TANGIBLE UNDER-STANDING THAT LIFE IS SHORT, AND WE ARE IN THIS FOR THE LONG-TERM . . . WE BOW OUR HEADS AND ACCEPT. . . .

Holidays and special occasions are a mix of emotions every year for bereaved parents. Many are shocked that these emotions recur year after year. However, listen to the same family one year later at Christmas now with a new ten-month-old daughter in their family.

As her first Christmas approaches
We find ourselves looking forward
Not so much back, with sorrow and longing

Don't misunderstand
There is still a stocking missing on the mantle
The Christmas family picture is incomplete
Fabric remains for one matching Christmas dress left uncut

But life does go on, after all
And for every painful reminder of what could have been
The Christmas promise brings what one days will be
Returning her to us

Meanwhile, we content ourselves
With the shadows of a daughter lost
Reflected in the innocent countenance of
A daughter gained

SUPPORT GROUPS

Every year people throughout the world suffer loss. Tens of thousands of parents lose children. It often helps healing to know we do not mourn alone. We are all unique and may benefit from different types of support.

Your circumstance, personality, relationship investment, and how you have viewed and coped with past experiences will influence your recovery. You may have learned to live with the "Why" questions or may have answered some for yourself. Life no longer feels like it has no meaning—just new meaning. Your priorities and views may have changed. If you have not allowed the pain of adversity to destroy you, you may discover you are stronger. In addition to doing your grief work mentally, physically, emotionally, and spiritually you may be able to now reach out and help others.

Many have found appropriate opportunities to reach out through support groups. Many have claimed it was very helpful, even if they attend only a few sessions. There are community groups that offer support for many kinds of losses. Check with your local hospitals or phone directory for referrals. Seeing and hearing other's experiences might help you understand you are not the only one who has hurt deeply. Their words may also offer promise of recovery. This sharing together can bring comfort.

Listen how Shirley Ottman, a former newsletter editor for "The Compassionate Friends," and a former National board member started helping others through a support group,

> When your child died, you found yourself in a dark abyss, painfully groping your way, looking for a firm handhold in the slippery business of rebuilding your life—as all bereaved parents, siblings, and grandparents have done before you and will do after you. To say that finding positive resolutions for your grief is not easy grossly understates the reality of the process. It is so difficult, in fact that it is tempting simply to give up and remain stuck in the mire of self-pity or anger or sorrow or guilt or denial or false gaiety. Oh, how we humans love to follow the path of least resistance! Yet this so-called "easy" route contributes nothing to long term emotional, physical, spiritual, or mental health. Remaining stuck in any phase of the grieving process dooms us to an incomplete and unfulfilled life, something our children, our siblings, or our grandchildren would deplore had they lived.

> For several months after my daughter's death, I too, groped my way through shock, disbelief, denial, anger, and despair. I cried every day and every night, incapable of joy. I forced myself to smile at appropriate times when I was among friends, even to laugh a little if others were laughing; but my heart wasn't in it. I'm sure I seemed hollow and sad and maybe even pathetic to others as I forced myself

back into familiar routines—grocery shopping, answering correspondence, singing in my church choir, playing bridge with my group. Even so, I felt empty, bereft of any interest in life whatsoever. I dreaded the future, which seemed to stretch endlessly before me. I knew my own despair dampened the lives of other family members, but I seemed powerless to effect any change in my emotions or my attitude.

Finally, four or five months after my daughter's death, my husband and I attended a TCF support group. It took real courage to attend, for to do so required that we drive over the very place where my daughter died on the interstate highway. I cried as our car rolled over those significant few feet of cement. At the meeting I cried several times again—telling my story, listening to others, and hearing the words of the seemingly wise young woman who facilitated the meeting that night. I cried again on the way home, and again in bed that night. I learned that my family was not alone. Other families had endured similar tragedies; and what's more, they were surviving.

Some of those other parents and siblings had actually laughed during the meeting. I couldn't remember why. It must have been that someone said something funny. Imagine! They could laugh—and their laughter seemed genuine! Hope was born in my heart that night in the small seed blown into my heart from others' concern for us and the light breeze of laughter I recognized even though I could not then participate. That small seed began to grow—in my heart, in my mind, in my spirit, in my home, in my relationships, and finally in my community. Because of that small seed, planted by bereaved parents, siblings, and grandparents at a TCF meeting, I credit "The Compassionate Friends" for saving my life. I hope our chapter can now plant those seeds for others too [4, pp. 2-3].

I wish I could tell you that one morning you will wake up and all the pain will be gone. It may be this way for some, yet I have observed for most, the following is true,

> There was no sudden, striking, and emotional transition. Like the warming of a room or the coming of daylight. When you first notice them they have already been going on for some time [5, p. 71].

Hopefully you will feel recovery coming as you try many of the self-help ideas we share throughout this book. As you are moving along the road to recovery, you will be able to better make plans and decisions, also set and accomplish goals. You are gaining confidence in concentrating, communicating, and accepting the realities of your life. You are responsible only for your own thoughts, behaviors, and actions. You are becoming free of resentment, fear, anxiety, guilt, worry, shame, and anger. You maintain personal hygiene, and function at work, home, and socialize comfortably. You rarely feel lonely, isolated, and insecure. You may now look forward to leisure activities, friends, and daily living. Remember it takes years and hard work to accomplish this kind of recovery. If you condemn and criticize yourself and others for not being there yet, it may defeat your progress.

In my recovery, I found with time I could think about the death of my son without the intense pain. I never dreamed it would take so long, but slowly the healing began. I knew I was starting to heal when I could reach out to others. When I could speak again publicly with confidence. When the memories of Cam brought me some feelings of joy instead of all pain and sadness. The cycles of grief will still come and go for the rest of my life, yet with time and effort the symptoms softened and came less frequently.

In addition to all the self-help you can do, we recommend turning to God and his word for power beyond your own. In John 14:18 Christ says, "I will not leave you comfortless. . . ." Matt 5:4 "Blessed are they that mourn: for they shall be comforted" [2]. See Chapter 8 for more ideas.

HOW TO HELP OTHERS WHO ARE GRIEVING

Many who have lost a loved one are so hurt or angry that they won't allow others to help them. They may seem to avoid you (isolation) or hide their grief. Try to allow them time and space, while letting them know you're there. Avoid telling them how to feel, or expecting them to "get over it." They never will! (see Genesis 37:35 [2]). They may adjust, accept, and recover, but will never be exactly the same again. All the grief work in the world can't get them back to where they were before their loss. They may forever carry an "empty room" in their hearts [1, p. 152]. You may help them deal with their adversity best by understanding the following:

Don't try to minimize their loss by offering cliches such as:
1. You're young 2. You can have other children 3. Put it behind you

4. Time will heal everything 5. Be strong 6. Count your blessings 7. Only the good die young 8. Don't say you understand exactly how they feel because everyone is unique, and chances are you may not understand.

Don't be afraid of their pain, it's theirs not yours. Remember, someone who has lost a loved one will take it hard! Those who make small talk and fear mentioning the lost loved one often cause more hurt. Don't be afraid of causing tears by sharing memories of their loved one. Memories are all they have. Other children do not take the place of the one they have loved and lost. They generally don't hurt by choice, they are trying to recover, but it's often long hard work. Know that time moves painfully slow, it is very frightening for many to think of living the rest of their lives without their loved one.

I feel the following story shows how vulnerable we can feel for an extended period of time. And what others do to make us feel so out of place.

WHEN THE MASK FALLS OFF

Many special occasions following the death of our son have been bittersweet moments for me. In part I feel all the joy and love that these moments bring forth but on the other hand, always present is the heartache of missing him. How do I get through these moments without bitterness, anger, and despair? It's not easy and I haven't always been successful. In fact, on one occasion when the mask fell off, I went to pieces.

I expected to enjoy our nephew's wedding. My sister was particularly pleased that we had made the effort to share this occasion with them only a year after our son died. I was ready to enjoy the moment. As the service began, I leaned back, took a deep breath, and relaxed—my mind wandering. Suddenly I heard the minister say that the bride and groom wished to remember departed family members on their special day. How unusual, I thought. He mentioned grandparents and other relatives, and suddenly I heard the name of my son. I froze. NO! NO! Not my son, not a departed person, not dead, not gone. NO! NO! I stopped breathing. My eyes filled with tears. My body slumped in the pew. I mustn't cry, not here, not now. I had to control myself. Then the mask fell off. Oh Duncan, Duncan, my heart cried out. Please don't be dead. The dagger which is the full realization of his death always plunges deep when it attacks. Then it twists and turns, leaving my insides cut and ripped in agonizing pain.

I started shaking. My husband Gordon reached for my hand, but I couldn't be comforted. All too soon the service ended. The bride and groom floated by. I couldn't stop crying. Raising my eyes, I saw my sister stand. The tears were running down my face and splashing on my suit. Our daughter and her husband rose and stepped toward the aisle. I couldn't move. Gordon took my arm. I shook my head. How could I, with a face contorted in grief, join the happy congregation?

When everyone had left, my husband and I made our way slowly up the aisle. We saw the wedding party posing for pictures and stepped back into the church. Gordon said nothing. He understood. He didn't try to make me stop; he remained by my side—a caring partner. As the crowd dispersed, our daughter and her husband came to find us. The sight of her brought fresh tears to my eyes. When I looked up, she had stopped some distance away and was staring at me. There was no comforting hug or word. She looked very remote.

As we left the church, I apologized to my sister. "Well," she said, "they didn't mean to upset you!" She turned her back and stepped into the waiting car. I stood in disbelief. There was no understanding of my pain. My daughter had nothing to say except to offer the suggestion that I get counseling. Years later I would understand that I had embarrassed my daughter and sister. My frightening face, horribly swollen and red with bloodshot eyes peering out between puffed eyelids, would make it necessary for them to tell the story of our son's death to the wedding guests who didn't know us. It was too much for either of them to cope with in the middle of a festive wedding.

But at that moment, I could feel only anguish in my heart and hurt because I felt my loved ones had turned their backs on me. I was devastated. I hadn't meant for my carefully constructed mask to fall off. I wanted to be part of the festivities, but I felt I had ruined everything. Gordon and I left for the hotel and finally made the decision to skip the wedding reception and leave for home. I didn't want to go to the reception looking as I did. I didn't feel like seeing the family and they certainly didn't want to see me.

As we arrived at the airport, people stared at the distraught woman in dark glasses. I didn't care. Finally we were strapped into our seats and airborne. My husband took my hand. His understanding started the tears again. Looking up into the endless sky helped. I always felt closer to my son high in the clouds above earth. After we landed, we hurried through the airport, collected our bags, located

> the car, and drove back into our busy lives. We would go forward. I would be better. I would reassemble the mask and fasten it firmly on my face again, hoping that someday my splintered heart might be healed enough so that I could remove it forever [6, p. 5].

For many, the hardest part of recovery is realizing that few people can understand and relate to their pain. This causes hurt, anger, anxiety, and withdrawal. The best way you can help a grieving friend or relative is to just be there for them. They need to know you really care. You may have to work through some of your own feelings and fears before accepting theirs. The following feelings shared by those in grief may also help you understand and support them better.

> Let me talk about the death, feelings, memories over and over again. Call me everyday. Know that I feel scared and lost. Encourage me by telling me I'm doing good. Tell me it must be hard, and you can't imagine, or understand, but you're there for me anytime as long as I need it and then some! Tell me all my feelings, and fears are normal and it will take lots and lots of time and patience to heal. Understand I may not want to do anything social for a long time, but I still need you as my friend.

You can never listen too much. You may hear the bereaved say the same things over and over again. They need someone to be there and listen! You will not totally understand, don't worry about trying. Try not to make any judgments, just listen. Help them keep the good memories alive.

Also truthful positive reassurance that they, along with the doctors, hospital staff, etc., did all they could for their loved one. Parents are already carrying enough guilt and doubts. If you have experienced death, try to realize each loss is different to all of us, don't compare losses. Don't over-share your experiences, focus on their feelings. Don't run away or ignore their feelings. Don't preach or moralize. Offer all the acceptance and love you can. Never rush or push the bereaved into situations, places, or feelings they are not ready for. They will let you know when they are ready, and it may even surprise them how long it takes. Offer to go with them to a support group. Don't be afraid of causing tears. Don't try diverting conversations to other topics. Most bereaved want to cry, talk, and remember their child. It helps them do their "grief work." It is helpful to discourage them from making major decisions or changes for at least one year. Don't be afraid to appropriately touch them, touch can be a healing aid. Follow up regularly, not just the first weeks or months, but a year or two or more! It can help them do their grief work if they handle some of the plans and arrange-ments. Don't leave the bereaved "passive" by doing everything for them. They still need your support, not a "surrogate sufferer" [1, p. 21]. Doug Manning suggests "using the three Hs: Hush, Hug (if they'll let you!) and Hang around" [7, p. 25].

Those who helped us the most called, sent cards, and letters with comforting words, and tokens of their love. They listened, listened, and listened! We are especially touched and close to those who will still talk years later and remember him with us. We also feel good when people share with us how sorry they are because they love and enjoyed our son, and truly miss him too. Because we live so far from where our two children are buried, it has meant a lot that our families have put flowers and tokens of love on their graves without us even asking.

DO I NEED PROFESSIONAL HELP?

If depression, anxiety, guilt, or any emotion becomes debilitating, professional counseling or medication may assist you in your grief work. Most of us would not hesitate to go to the doctor to seek treat-ment for a physical illness. Yet many are hesitant to seek help when it comes to their mental and emotional health.

> Loss, grief, and mourning all assault the mind, the spirit, the heart and the body. They attack you in the personal, social, and work worlds. Going for professional assistance in grief does not mean that you are "crazy." It means that you are seeking what you need in order to resolve your grief and recover optimally from your loss [8, p. 307].

If you feel you could benefit from professional help, then that is reason enough to seek it out. An example would be with the common problem of depression. The DSM-IV classifies a depressive "syndrome" as having at least five of the following conditions for at least two weeks. (Since these symptoms would be normal for a major loss we might change the duration from weeks to months.)

> 1. A preoccupation with worthlessness or guilt 2. Diminished interest or pleasure in activities 3. Prolonged functional impair-ment 4. Psychomotor retardation 5. Sad or irritable mood most of the day 6. Five percent or more weight change 7. A change in sleeping patterns, fatigue 8. Unable to think or concentrate 9. Suicidal thoughts [9, p. 327].

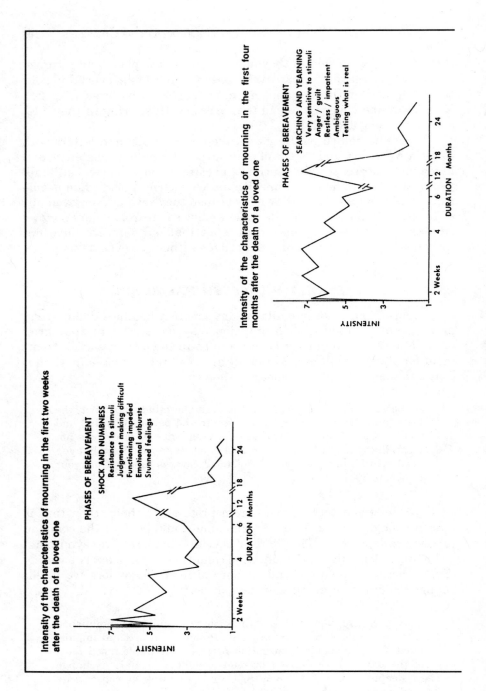

Intensity of the characteristics of mourning in the first two weeks after the death of a loved one

PHASES OF BEREAVEMENT

SHOCK AND NUMBNESS
Resistance to stimuli
Judgment making difficult
Functioning impeded
Emotional outbursts
Stunned feelings

Intensity of the characteristics of mourning in the first four months after the death of a loved one

PHASES OF BEREAVEMENT

SEARCHING AND YEARNING
Very sensitive to stimuli
Anger / guilt
Restless / impatient
Ambiguous
Testing what is real

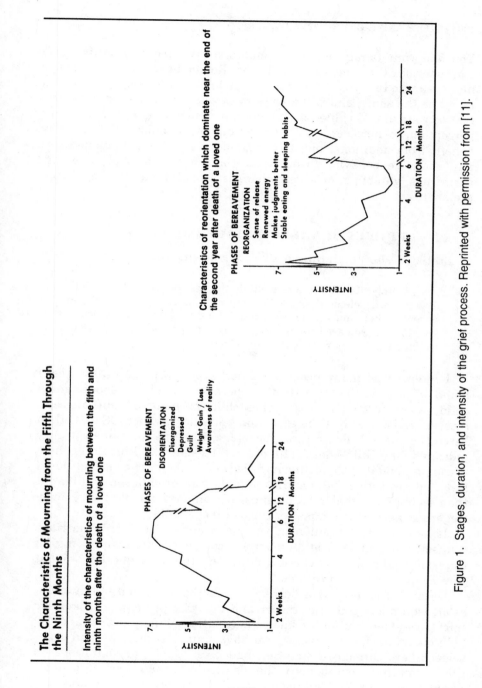

Figure 1. Stages, duration, and intensity of the grief process. Reprinted with permission from [11].

You and your family or close friends may be able to identify these characteristics in others or yourselves. Remember it can take two or more years to find your "new normal" and not feel so "empty." You will never be the same, and will always miss your loved one, probably the rest of your life. Yet, life has taken on new meaning with a different perception. If however, you cannot function or enjoy life, you may benefit from additional aid. If you think often of suicide or increase any addictive behavior through excessive use of alcohol, smoking, sex, drugs, gambling, or severe changes in eating habits, you should seek help.

PROFESSIONAL MARRIAGE COUNSELING

Statistics show high rates of divorce following the death of children.

> . . . healing after the loss of a child is never complete. There will always be an element of relationship missing in the heart of the parent. When you are seated across the dining room table from your spouse, you are looking into the eyes of a person who has been wounded. His or her life is still tinged with sorrow [12, p. 50].

I interviewed many people who had experienced several losses. I found as listed in the DSM-III, that those who had lost a spouse and a child, generally found the loss of their child was more difficult to accept, recover, and adjust to. (The exception was suicide which DSM-III then listed the spouse's death as catastrophic, which is the same category indicated for a child's death [10, p. 18].) It seemed so difficult for them to comprehend that their child had died before them. The unconditional love and protective feelings that parents feel for children is different than feelings in other relationships. It's understandable that a marriage may need extra help after the death of a child.

If your marriage is suffering you may want a professional marriage counselor. Remember not all marriage counselors are trained in grief counseling. It's okay to check around and then ask questions about your counselor's qualifications.

Because Dennis was a licensed psychotherapist and family counselor, we understood grief theory and the grief process. Although we hurt beyond description we knew many of the self-help tools that could help our marriage survive. As we have shared earlier, we had counseled others through their grief, had given public presentations on grief, and had experienced the deaths of grandparents, friends, parents, and our first infant daughter. However, it wasn't until the death of Cameron that we realized how little we understood about significant grief and its effects on a marriage (see Chapter 7).

Figure 1 is a graph of stages, duration, and the intensity of the grief process. It has helped us realize how long and hard the road to reconciliation can be. We also realized that we are not alone in our recovery [11].

REFERENCES

1. D. Edwards, GRIEVING: The Pain and the Promise, Covenant, Inc., Salt Lake City, Utah, 1989.
2. Authorized King James version, BIBLE, A. J. Holman Co., Philadelphia.
3. F. Nietzsche.
4. The Compassionate Friends of N. Texas, TCF Newsletter, 6:4, pp. 2-3, April 1993.
5. C. S. Lewis, A Grief Observed, Bantam Books, New York, 1976-88.
6. N. F. Doss, The National Compassionate Friend Newsletter, Oak Brook, Illinois, Spring 1993.
7. D. Manning, Grief is a Family Affair, In-sight Books Inc., Hereford, Texas, p. 25, 1991.
8. T. Rando, Grieving: How to Go On Living When Someone You Love Has Died, Lexington Books, Simon & Schuster, New York, 1988.
9. DSM-IV, Diagnostic and Statistical Manual of Mental Disorders (4th Edition), American Psychiatric Association, Washington, D.C., 1994.
10. DSM-III, Diagnostic and Statistical Manual of Mental Disorders (3rd Edition), American Psychiatric Association, Washington, D.C., 1987.
11. G. W. Davidson, Understanding Mourning, Augsburg Publishing House, Minneapolis, Minnesota, 1984.
12. L. Yeagley, Grief Recovery, Muskegon, Michigan, 1981-84.

CHAPTER 7

Our Relationships:
Marriage, Friends, and Family
(Other's Reactions to Our Loss)

Good relationships don't just happen, it takes hard work at all times. When you add loss, stress, grief, disabilities, and chronic or terminal illness to your relationships you may expect additional changes and challenges.

Dennis and I grieved differently over the same losses. We found it vital that we accept each others style and duration of mourning. We also learned we had to accept our family, friends, and others differing reactions to us and our losses.

Caring for a child with an illness, or coping with grief after his/her death, becomes physically, emotionally, and mentally exhausting. You may feel numb and find it hard to put as much time and energy into other people. Many relationships may be strained and different for a time.

Often grief can bring out the worst in us, our spouse, friends, or family.

> Some statistics indicate that as many as 85% of the marriages fail after experiencing the death of a child [1, p. 84].

> Other research reveals a 70% divorce rate for those parenting a disabled or chronically ill child [2, p. 208].

How can we prevent these secondary losses? How can we, in our grief grow to understand that the loss or illness of this child is profound, yet our life and commitment to relationships must go on?

How might we prevent divorce, loss of friends, and other secondary losses that can hurt our entire family?

We have presented marriage workshops over the years and have learned and experienced some basic principles that we feel helped us and others with various relationships after loss.

COMMUNICATION

We have found the most common reason couples dissolve their relationship is the inability to honestly and openly talk with one another. This lack of communication and planning together can bring on abuse, drinking, infidelity, or dissatisfaction with life in general. If a couple does stay together without good communication and shared feelings, it is as if they are living separate lives. They each go in their own direction keeping busy with responsibilities and activities without sharing what is needed to build a deep long-lasting relationship. Communication is especially difficult when you are exhausted or hurting, yet critically important in weeding out misunderstandings that arise during these emotional times.

Open communication is not only important for healthy marriages, but improves relationships with friends and family as well. Many of us think we are communicating, when in effect we are not being understood or listening in return.

> We must seek first to understand, then to be understood [3, p. 45].

If we are only pretending to listen while preparing our own reply, others may continue to feel misunderstood or give up entirely. When someone is truly listening and trying to understand us, we will often experience a sense of relief, love, and closeness. In return we may now be able to offer true understanding and attention.

We may not be willing to share if we feel condemnation or judgment. Generally a level of trust and a feeling of being safe and accepted encourages us to express our feelings freely.

One simple technique that has helped us, requires reflective listening. This technique encourages you to repeat back what was said before you express your own point of view. The sender of the message attempts to state what he/she feels and why, then the receiver clarifies by stating,

> You feel _____ about _____ because _____ [4, p. 3.3].

By using this technique you can avoid discounting someone's true feelings. Unfortunately this is often done by statements such as, "Yes, but." It is not healthy to tell someone they SHOULDN'T feel a certain way. (Have you seen the buttons some have worn, "Don't SHOULD on me!"?) People's feelings are usually there for a reason, and repressing or stuffing them rarely makes them go away. When we are allowed to feel and share our negative feelings we can often let them go. Reflective listening usually works well with friends, couples, children, and teenagers.

Being specific in your communication is important. If you really like something your children, friends, or spouse did, tell them, don't just wait and wonder why they don't do it more often. (If you never let your partner know it is important for you to get roses on special occasions you may never get them!) Don't assume others will figure out what your needs are, and if you neglect your own needs, often resentment results. Sometimes couples benefit by making a bargaining list. For example, I really like tasks done around the house and Dennis enjoys time spent watching TV together and having his back rubbed. We trade off, one night we get all the household and yard repairs done, and the next night we watch TV or a movie. This kind of compromising also works well with our young and adolescent children. However, it will likely never happen without honest and open communication. Some couples may have even forgotten what it is they would like their spouse to do for them. Many have to think back to their childhood or courting years to identify the things they used to enjoy. For a list of pleasing behaviors try the Spouse Observation checklist by Weiss, Patters, and Thomas (microfiche) (Princeton, New Jersey: Ed. Testing service.)

Specific communication may become damaging if we are using it to find faults. Is there such a thing as constructive criticism? If it must be done, do it lovingly and ask yourself if it will build your spouse, or just hurt. (At our house, we ask our children, "Did what you just said, build or hurt your brother or sister?")

Good relationships are not devoid of conflict. It is how one resolves the conflicts that makes a difference. Realize not all issues can be solved. We have learned sometimes you have to AGREE TO DIS-AGREE, and let it go.

During your grief you may find yourselves less patient and more annoyed and irritable. Avoid reading meaning into others statements, take time to stop and clarify. Many people will misinterpret a little comment made in passing and ruminate on it all day. They then feel hurt and ready to react or fight later over what may have simply been a correctable misunderstanding.

We found time spent weekly alone together without interruptions can increase understanding, love, and communication. If you are spending most of your time with work, hobbies, or other interests, you cannot expect your relationships to always go smoothly, especially with your marriage and family. The majority of your time and focus ideally must be directed toward those relationships to insure success. This requires a great deal of planning when families are grieving, or have the added responsibility of caring for an ill, or disabled child. If communication time together is limited, it may be helpful to write your feelings down before you come together and share them.

When you are finally communicating, avoid the trap of harboring unconfirmed negative thoughts and fault finding. Dennis and I would try to really listen to each other without judgments, defensiveness, or harsh words. It's hard to pull back negative words, and once you make a habit of saying them, it's hard to stop. We also tried to focus on the problem not the person, with kindness and compromise. The old saying of "act, don't react" usually works.

Cooperation and "giving in" can work miracles too. I learned if I always had to be right and "win," in the end I usually lost. And if you get into a power struggle with a teenager you are doomed to lose. Sincere apologies for our errors or misunderstandings will open doors the quickest. I try to "let go" of any pride or selfishness. I try to be FORGIVING, giving others the benefit of the doubt. It can be very helpful in building relationships.

Don't waste time wishing things were different, especially things that you cannot change. You can wish your whole life away. We can't really control or change others, only ourselves. "Letting be" or "letting go" of your need to control situations or others can bring more peace to you and those around you. In other words, cut others some "slack"!

TOUCH

There is great power in touch. Studies have shown animals (and infants) can die without sufficient touch and affection. Relationships are the same way. The right kind of touch can diminish anger, soften hurt, and help heal grief.

There are many different kinds of touch. Hugs, holding hands, a good-bye kiss, and sexual intimacy are all ways of showing our affection. Different kinds of touch are appropriate in different kinds of relationships.

When a couple is under stress or grieving, intimacy may be halted or changed. One partner may feel the need for intimacy and closeness as assurance that all is not gone. The other may see intimacy as an affront wondering how anyone could think of it at such a time. Research indicates it may take several months or years for some to readjust sexually after a traumatic loss.

As a couple we tried a new kind of touch that softened our pain, brought us closer together, and helped heal us in all dimensions of our relationship. We had understood the importance of different kinds of touch, but had never really taken the time or felt the need to implement this kind of touch—a body massage. It became a valuable healing and relaxation technique for our grief.

This type of touch does require some time and privacy [5]. Ideally you give each other ten to thirty minutes of massage time. You could talk during the session or do some slow deep breathing exercises as you meditate. Music also helps many people to relax. You may be surprised how grief and stress can cause your muscles to tighten and eventually ache. Sometimes you might use oil or lotion. (This type of touching generally does not include sexual intimacy, but could if a couple so desired.) If you add an overnight "motel getaway" from children and work, the healing may be more beneficial. Many of us don't take the time to relax our bodies or our minds in this manner.

Marital partners need bonding time to renew their commitment and nourish their love and trust for each other. This can be done through weekly dates, and affection on a regular basis. This does not just happen, it must be planned and scheduled just as those other important events in your life. Many have found it helpful to have a set weekly date night that both can count on. We were counseled by a religious leader many years ago that going into debt was not wise, except for purchasing a home and regular DATES! We decided we couldn't AFFORD not to date and court each other.

Our children needed our time also. We have found it beneficial to schedule time to be together each week also. Some also find it helpful to plan time with each child for a one-on-one activity and discussion.

MEN AND WOMEN ARE DIFFERENT: INCONGRUENT GRIEF

Partners may grieve and respond to the same situations in different ways. Often a couple feels they have lost their best friend (spouse), while grieving. The way a spouse or child responds to a death or illness may be confusing. Remember crying is not the only way people show pain. Society conveys differing expectations for struggling men, women, boys, and girls. It may be helpful to recognize and talk about these differences with patience and understanding toward one another.

Understanding the differences between men and women can enhance your relationships. Generally there are not only biological differences, but boys and girls are usually brought up differently from each other. For example, men are often encouraged not to cry as a symbol of their strength. They are taught to protect and provide. When their child dies, men often feel powerless and that they have failed in their role as "protector." As little boys, men are often taught to be strong and silent, while we may encourage little girls to express their emotions. Men are often not as interested in details as women. Most women tend to be more tender, nurturing, and interested in happenings at home. It's no wonder they lose their identity and may need more support when a child dies. Women are usually feeling and relationship oriented, while men are more factual, logical, and objective. Women are more romantic, men often more passionate. Women are often more talkative, jealous, and idealistic. Men may seem more secretive, conceited, and realistic. Women are generally intuitive while men are often concrete. Some have suggested that men grieve intensely for a short duration, while many women seem to grieve less intensely initially, yet may grieve over a longer time frame needing more support. When you add these differences to other variables such as family background, age, coping styles, personality, values and beliefs, you may see why patience with others is vital, especially during high stress times. Generally, many of these factors and differences attract and draw men and women together in healthy relationships. However, with the stress of illness or death, some of these differences may get in the way of stable relationships. There must be a wide latitude of acceptance, to avoid conflict. The following is a common example of how difficult it may be for some couples to cope with these differences.

My husband Jeff is a sensitive, though not talkative man. After Blake (their child) died, he told me "I will listen to you, but please don't expect me to talk. I just can't." Knowing me as he did, Jeff realized there would be no long silences in our home. Sure enough, when the poor man dragged in from a hard day's work, I pounced on him and chased him through the house, crying, questioning, recounting the terrible details of Blake's death. Usually I drove him into the bathroom, where behind a locked door, he could finally have some peace. I could outlast him though, and when he emerged, I was waiting for him, yammering non-stop. Ultimately, Jeff stopped listening to me altogether. I envied the fact that Jeff had somewhere to go each day. Some years before, we had agreed that I would retire from teaching temporarily until all the boys were in school. With nothing special to do, the long, empty hours stretched before me each day as I fulfilled my domestic duties, my mind never leaving Blake and our tragedy for an instant. One day I demanded to know how Jeff could just get up each day an go to work like nothing had happened. He replied, "Look, Pat, I'd like to lie in bed and cry all day, but if I did that, I'd lose my job, and where would that leave us?" I've always hated rational responses. Another area of animosity arose from our nocturnal habits. Despite the torment he was suffering, Jeff was still able to sleep. Night after sleepless night, as I lay there listening to his even breathing, I got madder and madder. How could he sleep when our precious boy was dead? I wanted to kick him—and did a couple of times. In my sleep, of course. As time passed, our relationship deteriorated. My kind, gentle husband, whom I could never provoke to fight no matter how I tried, was now snapping back at me or worse, ignoring me completely. To say that I resented him would be an understatement, and I can only imagine how he felt about the volatile harpy that used to be his loving wife. Finally, as if things weren't bad enough, we made plans to do something that sends the most blissfully married couple sprinting to divorce court: we decided to build a house. . . . After awhile it seemed to me that every good thing about our marriage was gone, and I doubted that it was worthwhile for us to live together anymore. Jeff must have felt the same way, but I was the one who said it aloud. If I live to be a hundred, I'll never forget his words to me. He said, "Pat, as much as Blake loved this family, how would he feel if he thought his death caused us to break up?" It was a low blow, but it brought me to my senses. I couldn't have my beloved Blake thinking he caused such unhappiness. Then and there, I committed myself to the restoration of our marriage. I vowed to stick to Jeff like a tick to a hound. The man would never be rid of me, even if he wanted to be. It wasn't all lollipops and roses from then on, but things got better. I began seeing a kind psychologist who didn't hide from me in the bathroom. I spent time talking with other bereaved parents. I went to work part-time. . . . Almost five years have passed since that horrendous day that altered our lives forever. Jeff and I are still together. And will be, for ourselves, for our surviving children, and for Blake. We'll make it [6, p. 1].

It can be very confusing when couples handle grief and stress differently. Each having expectations and needs that the other cannot always fulfill. Couples have to learn to cope with unmet expectations. One husband told his wife he was very bothered by the death of their child even if he didn't cry a lot. He had other ways of dealing with his pain. Another man at the support group I facilitate stated, "He had fully recovered from the death of their child and was only there to help his wife." This was very confusing to his wife because she was in such agony and it had been a short time since their child died. We shared with them that people do grieve differently and that their grief also varies in its duration. We also warned them that some who feel recovered prematurely, have in fact repressed their feelings and find themselves experiencing major depression or posttraumatic stress disorder many months or years later (re-experiencing the painful feelings) [7, p. 424].

Another mother who felt alone and misunderstood in her grief by her husband wrote the following letter to her deceased two year old,

> I think I would be able to handle things a lot better if I knew this baby was o.k. (she may be carrying a Down's syndrome baby, and already has one learning disabled child). Is it o.k.? . . . I keep thinking over and over of the night you fell. It breaks my heart! Am I missing something, am I forgetting something, did I do something wrong to make you die, to leave us? Why did we lose you? You were the best thing to happen to our family. The other two kids have had a lot of problems lately. What is to become of us? Can we ever feel peace and joy in this life ever again? It is so hard for me to talk to many people about my troubles. They don't understand. EVEN DADDY DOESN'T UNDERSTAND HOW I FEEL. I love you. Mom.

We often assure women that it doesn't mean their husbands do not love them or their child when they don't exhibit grief openly.

We must also recognize that men and women's bodies and brains are biologically different. This includes differences in hormones and the way our brains process information. There are theories on how men and women use their left and right brain differently; and theories of how men think differently from women. Some feel many women (I fit this) view themselves and their lives as a "whole." If they perceive a small flaw somewhere in their personality or conduct, they may then condemn the whole self harshly. This all or nothing thinking can be very damaging. On the other hand, men generally view their conduct and personality "compartmentally" (this fits Dennis). For example, if a man speeds to work or loses his temper, he still may view himself very positively as a whole. He is able to ignore his faults while focusing on the good characteristics ("compartments"), such as his role as a supportive father or hard worker. Men usually rationalize more and don't focus on their weaknesses as much as women do.

Although there are many who feel men have hormonal cycles, there is greater acceptance and evidence concerning women's cycles, and how they effect her mood, emotions, and feelings.

During the first week of a woman's cycle her level of estrogen rises. At this time many women feel positive, confident, capable, energized, and outgoing. By the second week the estrogen may fall slightly or even out. She then generally still feels optimistic, happy, cheerful, creative, and peaceful. At ovulation the estrogen and progesterone rise. She may feel more assertive and sexually aware, affectionate, and usually still happy, peaceful, and content (although some women say they feel a few days of moodiness around ovulation). At the third week estrogen rises higher than the progesterone. She may start to have mood swings at this time. She may be a little more irritable, introverted, and not feel as well or positive. In the fourth week estrogen and progesterone fall and this often brings an increase in moodiness, nervousness, and oversensitivity to stimulation. Some feel angry and note a loss of self-esteem. For many the list of negative feelings and emotions seems exhausting! If both husband and wife are aware of these biological changes, they can plan ahead. Realize that the stress of an ill child, or your grief may also increase these PMS (premenstrual syndrome) reactions [8, pp. 40-43].

Having realistic expectations for each other is important. We cannot be the same exact people or couple after a major loss. The event becomes part of us and our life's experience. It is very hard to give each other love and support when you are in so much pain yourself. Grief is an individual, singular process. It can't really be done completely as a couple. Time, patience, work, and knowledge can make a difference. If we understand the principles that help a marriage work, the differences between men and women, and grief theory we can work together more successfully. Also couples who are flexible and accepting of each other's differences can cope better and adapt more readily to these changes.

SURVIVING SIBLINGS

I was surprised to learn that approximately one in seven children will experience the illness and death of a loved one before they reach the teen years [1].

Some people feel children should be shielded from hearing about problems, death, and grief. They fear that it might be too hard for the children to understand or be too traumatic. Others believe children do not grieve and need not be involved in the illness, death, or funeral. We found these are myths. Most children do grieve and should be allowed to do so. Their grief may be different than that of an adult, or similar as they go through the grief stages. Their symptoms may be slower in surfacing, or even recur later when they reach young adulthood. ". . . Available evidence suggests that not to assist the bereaved child in actively dealing with the death is to predispose him to significant pathology and life long problems" [9, p. 155].

Generally children are resilient to emotional damage, they have periods of grief mingled with play. In fact, it is often through play that they do their grief work. They may watch and wait for their parents to do their own grief work first. You do not need to pretend to be happy for your children. Honesty is important.

Often children are not told their sibling is ill or dying. Children often sense the tension. If you are not communicating openly with a child, it may inhibit his level of trust in you. They may need help understanding how someone became ill or died. They may need honest reassurance that they or you will not get ill or die too. Seeing your grief helps them understand their own emotions.

Avoid making analogies that the deceased "went to sleep," or that "God took or needed her," this may be confusing for children. They may feel anger at God or at their religion because the child may feel they "needed" the loved one more than God. It's okay for children to learn life is full of problems and grief, and to know you may not know all the answers. If you make up answers or use cliches to comfort them now, when they become adults they may turn to those same antidotes and ultimately realize they are not always accurate or helpful. They then may become angry or disappointed with you and/or God. Be honest with them from the beginning and then they can begin to learn how to cope and prepare for adulthood. You can be a role model to help your children face life's challenges.

Realize you may need breaks from your children, especially during long-term illness or grieving. You may be surprised that you become angry, irritated, and lose patience more than usual under grief and stress.

Most children can choose to attend their siblings funeral. Explain what they may see and hear and let them decide if they'd like to attend or stay at home. Attending may help them realize and actualize the loss and allows them to grieve with others, say good-bye, and find some closure.

We knew our youngest child, who was almost three years old, could not sit still for the service. We asked another adult to sit in the foyer with her. She had attended the viewing prior to the service. She struggled with accepting that the body in the casket was the brother she had shared a bedroom with for three years. She yelled, "It is not Cameron!" Later, she did not want to view the pictures of him at the funeral either. We tried to explain that we felt it was his outer body or shell that was in the casket. We shared with her our beliefs that the spirit or personality never dies. At first this was a hard principle for her to grasp. We then used a cocoon and butterfly and also our hand in a glove to help convey our belief that the body and soul separate at death. These illustrations seemed to offer the comfort and understanding she needed. It wasn't long before she was interested in the funeral pictures and more details. She initiates conversation about Cameron often, now years after his death.

Usually children under two years of age cannot understand death as final, yet are becoming aware of separation. Even infants can sense distress or change in the home environment. Some may react by crying, a change in eating, sleeping, or bathroom habits. Others may withdraw or have a temporary developmental delay. Many cry when you leave them with someone else at first, but usually begin to play and be happy shortly after you're gone. If they have consistent nurturing from other significant persons in their life, they should recover from loss quickly.

For children between the ages of three and five, separation may still seem temporary. They may repeatedly ask surprisingly open questions after a loss. Or they may show indifference. They need love and assurance. They may enjoy time together reading and need extra hugs. They may also react with anger, fear, or guilt, occasionally feeling they caused the death. They may even act out with emotional outbursts or play "death" when they play "house."

Children age six to nine often view death as irreversible, and its permanence is starting to sink in. There may be denial or anger as with pre-teens. Honest reassurance about your love and their future will assist them in their grief work and build trust. They may be afraid or have nightmares. As they try to understand the meaning of death, they may still feel it couldn't happen to them. They may also act out with emotions, or poor behavior and grades at school. Or they exhibit physical symptoms like teens and adults often do.

Children ages ten to twelve generally understand death as final and may feel some blame and responsibility for the death. They may kid and joke about death to hide their fears and anxiety. Grades or behavior may become a problem at school too. Any age child may react with physical complaints and problems.

A teen may get depressed and withdraw, and experience grief similar to an adult, or they may become so involved with themselves and their own world, that they honestly do not feel deep grief. It would be confusing and generally unhelpful to push someone into expressing something they do not feel. It does not mean they do not love the deceased. Some know death can happen to them and they are desperately trying to understand the meaning of life. Avoid lectures, comparing, over control, and power struggles. Many have formed personal philosophical or religious views of illness and death. Teens may still be drawn to activities that involve risk-taking behaviors. They may participate in these activities with confidence feeling safe and secure with their future. Others have gained adult perceptions about death and its consequences.

Some teens are hurt because others think their parents are the only ones that are grieving. Many are afraid to show their grief, even to their parents who may have become over-protective. Some are fearful of the intense emotions they are forced to feel at this young age, and they're afraid of the future, worrying about the possibility of more loss.

Give all children as much information as they can comprehend. Let them know what to expect. Allow them to ask questions, over and over again. Share your feelings, memories, pictures, letters, etc. Try to provide a secure nurturing atmosphere even as you display your own emotion and grief. Encourage children to talk and express their feelings. Practice good listening skills. They could also express their grief by helping you make a memorial. It might offer comfort and closure for them to choose something special that belonged to the deceased that they could have as a keepsake.

Respect their feelings and privacy. Try to provide a stable family environment, making only necessary changes as you all work toward healing.

Sometimes the many changes siblings face are more significant over time than the actual loss of their brother or sister. These are considered secondary losses. It may mean a move, new friends, a different bedroom, or school. Mother may return to work, or change jobs, etc. You may want to let their friends, teachers, and school counselors be aware of their new circumstances.

Let children know death is a normal part of life. Death is sad, and hard, yet it is part of this earth life. Let them ask their questions, then ask them what they think, and how they feel. Speak at their level and respond with simple honest answers. Help them work through their grief, utilizing art, play, music, writing, reading, dance, or exercise. It's also a normal part of young children's grief work to act out death or a pretend funeral.

Sometimes it may appear that your children are not grieving. We tried encouraging our surviving children to talk to us. Some may bond with other children who have had similar experiences in a sibling support group. As adults we have more support from others whom have experienced loss. Our teenager's friends usually have no clue what grief entails yet. Support groups are available in most areas. Sibling groups are often available through the Compassionate Friends locally and on a national level. Check with your local hospitals, phone directory, or doctor for referrals. There is also reading material available especially for bereaved children.

We had four other children and they each grieved differently. However, we found death and loss could be explained to any age child. One of our sons wanted to talk, another felt we brought up his brother's death too often. He did not want to discuss it much at all. (Many are concerned they will upset their parents more.) It wasn't until a year and a half later that he shared his perceptions in a paper he wrote for school. It helped us understand how he felt and how he grieved his brother's death. Ultimately, he went through many of the same stages of grief we had experienced, especially as he matured. We felt and sensed his feelings of guilt and helplessness, when he wrote the following at seventeen and a half years of age.

> The death of my brother Cameron was one major event that had a dramatic effect on me. Cameron was fourteen years old and unable to walk all through his life due to cerebral palsy. The cerebral palsy effected the muscle coordination in his body. Mentally he functioned normally, but his movements and speech were hampered. Cameron was the second oldest in a family of five children. At the time of his death I was sixteen. I had a brother twelve, and one almost eight. My sister was almost three.

> Cameron was scheduled to have surgery for his legs which would hopefully allow him to move around more freely. The surgery like most, had some element of danger, yet the doctor performing the surgery had not lost any of his patients in seventeen years of practice.

> The surgery was performed and at first seemed to be a success. It was during the recovery period, the second night that complications arose. It was about 1 A.M. May 23, I'll never forget that night.

> I was sleeping in my bed when I was awakened, probably by the voices of my parents in the family room. I got out of bed and walked to the end of the hall ,where I heard them conversing about

Cameron. I knew then what had happened. At first I went back to my room afraid to talk to my parents. (Often children are confused with death and cannot understand their part in it.) I then decided to go back into the family room. I remember sitting on the couch and listening to my parents crying. I didn't cry right then for some reason, I just sat there staring at some balloons which had "get well soon Cameron" written on them. (Some children wait until things are better to express their pain.)

The next day things seemed only to get worse. As more people called or came over I became more angry and depressed. I still couldn't believe what had happened. I just wanted to speed my life up about two years and forget what had happened. (Denial, fear, unable to verbalize until later—maybe when cognitive skills were more developed.)

Cameron had been a very loving and caring brother. He impressed me by his ability to look at the positive side of things, even when things could be so negative. Cameron was always laughing and smiling. The little things we take for granted gave him satisfaction. He never got down on the fact that he couldn't do things, and that quality I'll never forget.

Darren expressed his guilt about remembering only one time he had done something really special for his brother before his death. He had promised Cam the first ride alone in his car after he got his driver's license. On his sixteenth birthday he rushed home with license in hand, and in front of all his friends, picked up Cameron and took him on the first ride. Cameron was thrilled, yet Darren felt he didn't do enough of these kinds of acts for his brother. This type of guilt is common among siblings.

Another sibling age twelve also suffered guilt for not being as kind as he wished to his deceased brother. He wrote in his journal:

I feel bad for all the times I put him down, but I am glad we got some neat things in too. He was may favorite brother and still is. At least we had some fun together and that's what counts. Cam I love ya . . . you're my # 1 man.

Our eight year old needed to be reassured of our love and that we were going to be there for him. We tried not to discount his fears and insecurities. His coping skills were not as mature as our other boys, nor did he share his feelings as easily. He did express guilt like the others, wishing he had been kinder to Cameron. We had to monitor his behavior and look for clues to help us know how he was doing.

Some behaviors to watch for in children who are stressed are "acting-out," regression, or other strong emotions. Also look for changes in eating, sleeping, or playing patterns. Some children may withdraw or complain of stomach aches or headaches.

If the deceased child is ill for a long time, with remissions and relapses, it is normal for children as well as adults to detach themselves before the death occurs (anticipatory grief). It is difficult for siblings as well as parents to endure the "letting go," and "holding on" again and again. Some may actually detach too early in an attempt to avoid this painful cycle of ups and downs associated with remissions and relapses.

The surviving siblings may not have received your time and attention. They may have lacked quantity, as well as quality time. You may have not been able to discipline them as consistently or as fairly as you would have liked. These are normal occurrences, however it may add to the guilt you feel, as well as the siblings.

If you feel you or your child are not resolving grief, or you are leaning on your children too often or too long for their support, try attending a support group or seek professional help.

Keep in mind that for some siblings the task of watching their parents and sibling suffering brings a myriad of confusing feelings for them. Research indicates that in some instances,

> The siblings of dying children may suffer just as much, and at times even more, than the ill children themselves [9, p. 407].

Remember, it may be confusing for children if you don't show or express your guilt and other emotions. It is generally healthy for children to see your distress, because it allows them to confirm some of their own fears and feelings. Remember FEELING IS HEALING. Children learn to trust from your behaviors. They may need reassurance that the depth of your grief or concern for the deceased does not lessen your love for them. They may need more touching and hugs. They may "act out" in many ways requiring your patience with their behaviors.

As mentioned earlier, most children (ours included) have not been as kind or patient with their dying sibling as they would have liked. They may have also felt ashamed or embarrassed by how their sibling looked or acted. They may have felt their sibling was "too good" and it should have been them that died. They may have "wished" their terminally ill sibling would have died sooner and wonder if such a "wish" caused the death. Reassure them that wishes, fighting and negative feelings between siblings are common and do not cause death.

It is common for parents to idealize the child who died (we did). If we verbalize these feelings too often it may cause our other children to feel they cannot measure up to the deceased. As a result of these feelings they may become angry or suffer more guilt feelings. They may also fear that they or other loved ones will die soon as they come to grips with their own immortality.

I worried constantly that my other children were not getting enough of my time while I cared for Cameron. I realized that "quality" time was important, yet all children need "quantity" time from parents too. They did make some sacrifices and I told myself it taught them patience. They complained at times, we found open communication at weekly family meetings helped us solve some of our problems. Dennis taught me to avoid "power struggles" by agreeing with the children's accusations or complaints by saying, "You may be right," "probably so," or "thanks for sharing that." There wasn't much they could argue about when we acknowledged their feelings and recognized their point of view. At times, these responses would help us all lighten up, laugh, and see things more clearly.

HOW DO WE KNOW IF A SIBLING NEEDS MORE HELP?

Knowing if you or your child needs professional help may not be easy to determine. We all grieve and recover differently. When children experience a traumatic event it is normal for any behavior to regress or become exaggerated. This can occur with the death or serious illness of a sibling. However, it is not healthy when natural emotions like fear, grief, anger, or jealousy become exaggerated and completely intrusive without periods of relief. If fear turns to anxiety or panic attacks, or if anger turns to rage, or if guilt turns to shame, or sadness to long-term depression, seek professional help. (Approximately 2% of children, and 5% of teens suffer clinical depression in the United States alone [10, p. 8].) Also when distorted emotions like fear of failure, rejection, shame or self-pity cause prolonged depression, bitterness, guilt, or anger, then you may need to seek professional help. Other warning signs may be the absence of grief, trying to replace the deceased, taking on a caregiving or grown-up role, or prolonged dysfunction at home, school, or work. Also seek professional help if your children show signs of destructive, addictive, or suicidal behavior.

HUMOR–EQUILIBRIUM

Trying to maintain an organized "happy home" with illness and death is not an easy task. I learned over the years I couldn't do everything I desired to do. I had to set priorities and let some things go undone or find someone to help me. I would have hired out help for the housework if I could have afforded to do so. Instead I delegated household chores to my other children. Things were never done quite the way I would have liked, yet I realized it was better than not getting chores done at all. I would have loved to hire a cook, yet I learned how to fix quick nutritious meals that were easy for Cameron to eat. This usually ruled out soups and we rarely had spaghetti. We would tease and laugh with Cam after he would try to eat long spaghetti noodles because he would be covered with the red sauce all over his face and nose! He hated wearing a bib, yet knew at times it was necessary. I was surprised the other boys learned to cook simple meals too! They also learned they would have to ride their bikes many places because of the time and effort required to take everyone to where they needed to be. We tried to be involved in as many family activities as we could and still find balance.

As the mother I always took the role of helping us keep organized and on time. I took this pretty serious at times. However, Dennis kept me in check. He humored us through many things. His fun nature would help us not take things too serious. This encouraged us to avoid discouragement and depression.

Cameron's personality seemed to develop into a nice blend of seriousness and sense of responsibility, mixed with a great sense of humor and teasing. He and his dad could laugh and tease each other through many hard times. What fun they had. When Cameron would agree with something that was being discussed, he would jokingly reply with a word he had learned to say pretty clearly, "Bingo"! This cheerful disposition was greatly missed after his death.

Finding humor and laughter with an illness or death may take time and work. At first we may laugh because were tired of always crying, yet it may not feel like real laughter. Over time we will find we can replace the deep pain with happiness and joy for living.

GRANDPARENTS AND RELATIVES

When grandparents discover their grandchild has a chronic or terminal illness, or has died, their loss is double. They lose a legacy as well as the pain they suffer watching their own adult child hurt and grieve. Many times the grandparents are ignored as they grieve alone with minimal support. They, too, will experience the grief cycle, and may benefit from support groups and grief education. They often are expected to comfort and be the main support for their adult child. This can be impossible or difficult at best for many. One grandmother, Margaret Gerner writes,

> I am powerlessness. I am helplessness. I am frustration. I sit here with her and cry with her. She cries for her daughter, and I cry for mine. I can't help her. I can't reach inside and take her broken heart. I must watch her suffer day after day and see her desolate. I listen to her tell me over and over how she misses Emily, how she wants her back. I can't bring Emily back for her. I can't even buy her an even better Emily than she had, like I could buy her an even better toy when she was a child. I can't kiss the hurt and make it go away. I can't even kiss a small part of it away. There's no bandage large enough to cover her bleeding heart. . . . I see this young woman, my child, who was once carefree and fun loving and bubbling with life, slumped in a chair full of agony. Where is my power now? Where is my mother's bag of tricks that will make it all better . . [11, p. 1]?

When we were first struggling to find out if something was wrong with Cameron as an infant, we felt his grandparent's and relatives anxious concern. When we finally got the diagnosis, they like us, assumed it was something he could grow out of, or work hard and recover from. We like most families, didn't think it could happen to us!

Each month they would ask how Cameron was doing, wanting to know what he could do and if he was progressing. Each time we would try to explain the small changes we would see. With time and education they came to realize as we did, that although we may see progress in some areas, he would never crawl or walk. As he grew larger, and time passed they learned to love and accept Cameron as he was. In fact, his grandparents and close relatives became some of his dearest friends, offering love, strength and support.

When he died they also mourned his loss and cried with us. Though many relatives may not have totally understood the depth and duration of our pain, many sent love and concern for us across the many miles that separated us.

This is not the case for everyone. Many couples feel their relatives do not try to understand, or don't know how to offer support. They may remain in denial for a long time. The Taylors felt their family was unaccepting. They would not believe the diagnosis and would suggest more testing, different doctors, and special vitamins. They may have meant well, yet not accepting the diagnosis may make you feel your child is also unacceptable. Soon you may feel uncomfortable and withdraw into social isolation. The Taylors found, like many have, that statements such as, "She'll grow out of it," doesn't help parents feel better or face the future [12, p. 31].

Educating relatives seems to be the key, yet not an easy task. One mother complained,

> It's hard to tell your mother, who has spent your whole life mothering you, that you know more about your kid's condition than she does . . . actually, it's not so hard to tell her—it's just hard to get her to listen! [12, p. 32].

In spite of the hardships, don't give up! Continue to tell your relatives about your child and share your feelings. It may ultimately help them, your child, and you, to share the details of your child's condition so their understanding, or grief work can pace your own. They may never understand as soon, or in the way you would like them to, yet the help they may offer could make a significant difference for you and your child.

FRIENDS

How do you help relatives or friends who are hurting for you deal with their hurt or grief and feel comfortable around you? Many of us hurt so much we push friends away. At first you may not feel like being with your friends, however, with time you probably will again. Let them help you if possible. Hopefully, a true friend will stay by your side and listen to your pain as long as you hurt. They may not completely understand, yet they may be willing to listen and accept your deepest, darkest fears and feelings. Invite them to cry with you when possible. If you can, let go of your fear that others might judge you or your child negatively. Share all you can with them, it can help you both.

Remember, education and accurate understanding of the illness, or the grief cycle, can benefit everyone. It is likely that some do not really know what you are facing, and until you can give them details or facts, they may feel uncomfortable around you. If you choose not to talk and share, they may never know how you are feeling. They are then lost as to how to help you or themselves. Don't keep your pain all to yourself. Others love you and are hurting too. Often they aren't sure what to do. Share and allow them to help lift your burdens.

FINDING MEANING–A POSITIVE ATTITUDE

A positive outlook (when there is little positive to see) can help your relationships as well as your life. Pearl Buck, when trying to process the fact that her daughter was mentally handicapped, asked,

> Why must this happen to me? She answered her own question with, "To this there could be no answer and there was none . . . my own resolve shaped into the determination to make meaning out of the meaningless, and so provide the answer, though it was of my own making . . . her (daughter's) life must count [13, p. 26].

V. E. Frankl, a Jew in the Nazi concentration camp learned,

> . . . to live is to suffer, to survive is to find meaning in the suffering. If there is a purpose in life at all, there must be a purpose in suffering and in dying. But no man can tell another what this purpose is. Each must find out for himself . . [14, p. 9].

I think the following quote helps in the process of finding our own answer to "why."

> He who has a why to live for can bear with almost any how [14, p. 85].

Alan McGinnis writes

> . . . tough-minded optimists approach problems with a can-do philosophy and emerge stronger from tragedies. . . . Indeed, recent studies suggest that upbeat people do better in school, are healthier, earn more money and maybe live longer than pessimists [15, p. 17].

Mr. McGinnis reminds us Thomas Edison in 1914 lost a million dollars worth of equipment and most of his work in a fire. Edison was quoted as saying,

> There is value in disaster. All our mistakes are burned up. Now we can start anew [15, p. 17].

How do you do this when your whole life seems to be in shambles? V. E. Frankl comments,

> We had to learn . . . that it did not really matter what we expected from life, but rather what life expected from us. We

needed to stop asking about the meaning of life, and instead to think of ourselves as those who were being questioned by life—daily and hourly [14, p. 85].

His father, mother, brother, and wife were killed in the gas chambers. In addition to these emotional losses he suffered a great deal physically. However, he found that even though his captors could torment his physical body, he still had control of his mind. He wrote,

> . . . they offer sufficient proof that everything can be taken from a man but one thing: the last of the human freedoms—to choose one's attitude in any given set of circumstances [14, p. 75].

He found a reason for "being, not doing." He explains that there were those who chose to comfort others and survived because of their positive attitude and because of how they chose to view and then define their circumstances.

Dennis taught me years ago that the way we feel is often a direct result of what we have been thinking about. When we are down and discouraged we should ask, "What have I been telling myself?" Even in our grief work, we must put a "limit on our worry." We must strive to spend the better part of each day thinking positive thoughts about ourselves, others, our spouses, our children, and our lives. We must find some positive things to dwell on if we want to feel good.

> Be not defeated twice; once by circumstances and once by oneself [16, p. 11].

(This concept does not discount grief work, meditation time or "inner child" insights [17] where we pull up and recall some of our repressed negative past in order to "feel and heal.")

A positive attitude can influence many, including your spouse and children. If you can say a kind or complimentary word to someone (honestly) it can help you and them feel more positive and loved. Our whole family looks forward to Dennis coming home, his fun cheerful personality brightens and encourages us.

We can change our behavior by altering our thinking patterns. We can also change our thinking patterns by altering our behaviors. These changes require hard work and effort. Sometimes we may need a professional to help us identify why we chose to think the way we do, and uncover some of our erroneous thinking patterns and negative labels. We always have a choice and agency [18, p. 12]. Understanding some of these kinds of thought processes may offer relief and improve our behavior as well as our thinking.

Others have expressed relief from their negative feelings or thoughts by trying to feel, focus, and then show, and express gratitude for the positive things in their lives.

I attempted to look for the positive things in my new life and my new identity. It wasn't easy, however, I discovered with time I could reach out and help others who were just beginning their grief journey.

REFERENCES

1. N. Cychol, *Pediatric Nursing Symposium,* Children's Medical Center, Cook County, Fort Worth, Texas, 1992.
2. F. Kupfer, *Before and After Zachariah,* Delacorte Press, New York, 1971.
3. S. R. Covey, *Principle-Centered Leadership,* Summit Books, New York, 1990.
4. *Becoming a Better Parent,* L.D.S.S.S., Salt Lake City, Utah, p. 3.3, 1976.
5. C. Schultz, *The Sexual Adjustment of a Bereaved Couple,* audio tape #CF10, The Compassionate Friends, Oak Brook, Illinois.
6. *The National Compassionate Friend Newsletter,* Oak Brook, Illinois, and P. B. Dyson in the *Beaumont Newsletter,* October 1992.
7. DSM-IV, *Diagnostic and Statistical Manual of Mental Disorders* (4th Edition), American Psychiatric Association, Washington, D.C., 1994.
8. J. Lush, *Emotional Phases of a Woman's Life,* Revell, Grand Rapids, Michigan, 1987.
9. T. A. Rando, *Grief, Dying and Death,* Research Press Co., Champaign, Illinois, 1984.
10. *Special Report Home Library,* Whittle Communications, Knoxville, Tennessee, 1993.
11. M. H. Gerner, *The Bereaved Grandparent,* Centering Corp., Omaha, Nebraska, 1990.
12. R. Simons, *After the Tears,* Harcourt Brace Jovanovich, Orlando, Florida, 1985.
13. P. S. Buck, *The Child Who Never Grew,* Woodbine House, Bethesda, Maryland, 1950.
14. V. E. Frankl, *Man's Search For Meaning,* Simon and Schuster, New York, 1946.
15. A. L. McGinnis, *The Power of Optimism,* Harpersanfrancisco, San Francisco, California, 1990 (reprinted in *Reader's Digest,* pp. 17-21, 1991).
16. B. L. Top and W. C. Top, *Beyond Death's Door,* Bookcraft, Salt Lake City, Utah, 1993.
17. J. Borysenko, *Minding the Body, Mending the Mind,* Addison-Wesley Publishing Co., Inc., Reading, Massachusetts, 1987.
18. C. Thurman, *The Truths We Must Believe,* Thomas Nelson, Nashville, Tennessee, 1991.

CHAPTER 8

The Role of Spiritual Healing

After Cameron's death I wanted to more than just believe he still existed, I wanted to know! The shock and pain I had felt when we received his diagnosis as an infant, was now tenfold! How could he be gone? Why now, he was so young, why, why, why?! I felt as Jacob mourning for Joseph who "refused to be comforted" [1, Genesis 37:35].

Over the years as Cam's mother and caretaker, I had learned to accept his problems, love him intensely, and even found joy and purpose in caring for him? I had spent nearly everyday for fourteen years . . . feeding, bathing, dressing, and getting him to doctors. He had special schools and therapy. He was happy and loved living. I was a pediatric nurse and felt I was doing a good job of caring for him. I had spent hours worrying and trying to find the right wheelchairs, computer, typewriter, electric bed, prone standing table, therapy, and school programs. And for what? Now he's gone, dead!

LIFE'S IRONY

I learned that unexpected, uncontrolled, or undeserved suffering happens. Even when our plans are good, and we think we have worked hard, things go wrong. All my work, planning, hope, and prayers for Cam's improvement from surgery seemed in vain. Even the neatly woven incisions on his hips, as he lay lifeless seemed mockery to my plan and organization. His beautiful eight-day-old electric wheelchair (which took a year of hard work to obtain) sat motionless.

I knew I had faith, believed in God, and in life after death. Yet in the beginning I was shocked to find my faith alone was not enough to comfort me. I felt Cameron's soul still existed, yet when I saw his lifeless body on that cold hospital gurney I wanted to know, not just hope that he was well and happy somewhere. I questioned intensely, as did Job, "If a man die, shall he live again?" [1, Job 14:14].

FAITH AND SPIRITUAL INJURY

As I reached out, I discovered I was suffering spiritual injury. In Webster's dictionary faith is defined as a belief or trust. The King James Bible dictionary says, "Faith is to hope for things which are not seen, but are true." Paul said in Hebrews 11:1, "Now faith is the substance of things hoped for, the evidence of things not seen" [1]. I still had faith, so why was I experiencing spiritual injury?

I learned that when adversity strikes, many turn to their faith or beliefs for strength and comfort. Some unbelievers find the POWER of faith and are strengthened by their trials and report their adversity turned them to God. Unfortunately it is also common for others of all religions to question their spirituality, faith, or beliefs during profound grief. They may feel hurt or angry that God did not protect them from their tragedy. They may also feel hurt or anger that their church family didn't understand the intensity or duration of their pain. Listen to one mother's feelings, as she writes to her deceased child,

> I finally went through my "angry" stage of grief. I have a close friend at church who said, "At least your new trial has probably taken the focus off of your grief for your daughter's death." She will never know just how wrong she was! I think of you constantly, of your normal birth, of how healthy you were. How you off-set the pain we sometimes feel with your brother's disability. I am so angry you had to die. I wouldn't be going through any of this if you were alive. My faith has wavered!

Often untrained clergy and well-meaning congregations are at a loss as how to accept and support someone experiencing such suffering. They often do a great job during the illness, at the funeral, and for several weeks after, offering meals, time, attention, and love. Unfortunately most individuals cannot understand that the mourning of a significant loss may take months, and often years for full recovery. Those in grief often feel unaccepted, confused, or judged, fearing that if they don't heal quickly they may be considered weak, unworthy, or unfaithful. As they pull away, they often add guilt to their list of emotions. They may now fear that they are not only turning from others and their faith, but from God. Because having faith is a sense of belonging to God, and is often felt through God's family and servants, mourners may feel great spiritual rejection during their grief. The isolation compounded by these negative emotions are usually of no benefit to the bereaved, or their church. I have heard we often bury more people outside the church doors than in the ground when a death occurs!

One religious leader explains, the reason we need support or comfort from others, and our faith families is for "reassurance . . . our need for reaffirmation that God still does care for us, that God is still with us and that God is still forgiving and loving and merciful. Our world has crumbled and the one constant we need to be reminded of is the constancy of God's love, as shown in Jesus Christ" [2]. How do we find and use this POWER of faith, utilize the atonement, and receive spiritual healing?

In my grief I was confused as are many, who reason if they have enough faith, they won't hurt emotionally, physically, mentally, or spiritually. Or worse, that they will be protected from adversity and safe from grief and pain because of their faith. I came to realize the difference between grief and faith; religion and spirituality. I found it valuable to fully accept that it "rains on the just and the unjust" [1, Matthew 5:45]. It was healing to believe that God can and does intervene in our lives, and miracles do happen, yet, in most instances he allows natural laws to run their course. A good example is the bombing tragedy of the Oklahoma Federal Building. Many have asked, "Why did some victims survive and others die?" It was helpful for me to see that life or death in some instances depended on which side of the building they were in, and the kind of injuries they received. Others have asked, "Why does God allow good innocent men, women, and children to suffer?" It has been helpful for me to recognize that God will not, and man cannot take away the gift of choice (agency) he has given us. Yet, some people make poor choices that limit (freedom) and hurt innocent victims. However, God is always there to comfort and support us through these crisis situations. "I will not leave you comfortless: I will come to you" [1, John 14:18]. We must also believe that God is just and merciful and there will be accountability and punishment for those who use their agency inappropriately [1, Psalm 62:12, Romans 6:23, Deuteronomy 24:16, 2 Peter 2:4]. It has also been helpful to believe that those who die do not suffer, it is those left behind that miss them, hurt, and grieve [1, I Corinthians 15:55 & 56].

DIFFERENCES IN FAITH AND GRIEF

I learned there is a difference between faith and grieving.

It's like you're on a desert and you are dying of thirst, and someone says, "Yes, you can have a drink, but not for thirty years!" [3, p. 151].

Yes, we would see our son again, but how we missed him now! It still seemed like a long earth life to live without him, we were barely in our forties! We hoped our faith would never again be tried as it has with this loss.

I realized there were few people who could understand the intensity or duration of my grief. This made me hurt, angry, sad, and guilty on different occasions. I did not want to allow any of these emotions to drive me from my friends, family, God, faith, or church. With time, work, and patience, I, like many, found I could return with love and forgiveness to my friends, relatives, and faith family, who were unable to understand my grief. I was then able to offer help and support to others. By helping to educate others, it allowed them to be better prepared to reach out to those in grief without creating negative feelings. Many came to understand the natural grief process, it's duration and the difference between having faith and having a need to grieve.

DIFFERENCES IN SPIRITUALITY AND RELIGION

I like to define spirituality as the deep feelings, yearnings, and knowledge of your heart and soul. How you relate to Deity/God/ a Higher Power and your personal relationship with him. Your faith, hope, and belief in unworldly affairs. Your religion is where or how you nourish your spirituality. Organized religion will include a system of policies, practices, and beliefs.

One young widower found relief from his spiritual injury when he told his minister he "didn't even know about God any longer." What love and acceptance this widower felt when the minister (representing God) said to him, "I was not the first person to question nor would I be the last" [4, p. 203]. What a relief for him to find someone willing to listen and accept his confusion and pain without judgment. Because of this unconditional love, the widower, like many, started to nourish his faith again by returning to his church.

A mother, writing to her deceased child, begins to process, understand, grow, and heal from her tragedy as she comforts her son,

My child said to me the other day, "Mom, why do really bad things keep happening to us?" I have thought about this a lot. I realize I have learned some things from these experiences. First of all, bad things are going to happen to us. Life is unfair. We aren't exempt from more pain and trials because you died. However, things won't always turn out as devastating as when you died. Sometimes we can get through tough times with a happy ending.

Terry Anderson spoke on National Prayer Day May 6, 1993, after experiencing over seven years of captivity in a hostile country. While there, his father and brother died. He admitted that as a teenager he had considered himself agnostic. However, in prison he had requested and received an American Bible from his captors. As he studied scripture, trying to make sense out of what was happening to him he felt comfort. He concluded he was not being punished for his sins, nor was he being tried as Job. He came to discover that adversity comes to all of us, beyond our desires or control. He concluded that it was his inner spirituality and faith that sustained him through his great trials and grieving. He still relies on faith and prayer to help him forgive and let go of the anger and negative emotions that he struggles with from this adverse experience [2].

I found this same concept in Acts 14:22 [1], where we are counseled to endure our tribulation and grief with faith. I tried using this principle as a child. As a nine-year-old girl I had some childhood fears. When I shared these concerns with my parents, my father bought me a necklace with a mustard seed in it. There was a message inscribed on the box lid that the necklace was in. It said, "If ye have faith as a grain of mustard seed (which is one of the smallest seeds that grows into one of the largest trees) nothing shall be impossible unto you" [1, Matthew 17:20]. As a young girl, I relied on that principle to help me overcome my childhood fears. (I was fortunate to have a mother that allowed me to express many of my fears and feelings.) Now as an adult I looked to the principle of the mustard seed to help me cope with loss.

I began this faith search again by reading and studying many things. I was especially drawn to learn all I could about life after death. I tried to find every book I could read on dying and "Near Death Experiences" (NDE). Even Paul's "Near Death Experience" had meaning to me [1, 2 Corinthians 2-4]. I reviewed the accounts of over a hundred people, including a few in person who felt they had died, left this earth and returned. I desired to know what these people saw and felt to help me understand what Cameron had experienced, where he was, and what he was doing. The grief was so painful I felt I couldn't rely on what I had been taught, or previously believed. I wanted to start over, planting my mustard seed again to regain faith, hope, and knowledge.

THE NEAR-DEATH EXPERIENCE (NDE)

I was consumed with my research. I read and studied, learning that over eight million people have had NDEs [5]. Because of my medical background I was impressed that scientific approaches were used by some medical professionals to rule out hallucinations or brief psychotic breaks as explanations for NDEs. I found comfort in Dr. Raymond Moody's work. He had interviewed hundreds of people who had been diagnosed as clinically dead by medical doctors, and then returned to life to share their experiences. He determined there are many common elements to a true "Near-Death Experience" [6, Introduction]. It is not necessary to have all of the elements, however a person who is clinically dead or dying will experience many of them. These elements have been documented many times by physicians and nurses trying to resuscitate a patient's heart which had stopped beating. Sometimes, only minutes later, the patient's heart starts beating again and many can describe the details of their experience. (Some felt that no one would believe that the experience really happened, and do not discuss details until later.)

Love, Joy, and Knowledge

Almost all of those who experienced a NDE, claim they will never be the same. The feelings they are left with become very important to them. Many describe an intense love and joy that they have never felt before. Betty Eadie wrote, "I understood . . . that love is supreme. Love must govern . . . we must love ourselves" [7, pp. 59, 60]. Many say they have a strong desire to give more love, kindness, and patience to others. They have a thirst for knowledge. Most felt they have more meaning and purpose for living. They no longer fear death, yet sense they have important things to do before they die. Their life takes on a new purpose and mission.

Noise, Tunnel, Out of Body

Many find themselves traveling down a tunnel with vibrating sounds around them. Then they may find themselves outside their physical body, viewing it from above. This is not frightening, just a very interesting fact. Those who were in pain find the pain has left them. Dr. William Hunter, a dying physician in his last moments said,

> If I had strength enough to hold a pen, I would write how easy and pleasant it is to die [8, p. 52].

Those who return from death describe it similarly. Feelings of freedom, peace, and joy begin immediately.

One lady who had an NDE that I interviewed described her "fear" about leaving her husband, mother, and child behind on earth was replaced with comfort. She now understood somehow that it would be a short time until they could join her, and that they would be fine without her. She was very disappointed when she discovered she must go back. She returned to the hospital room, viewing her body from above as the professionals got her heart going again. She then returned to her body.

Nonverbal Communication, Light, and Life Review

Many see a light or spirit being that helps them review their life (some feel this is God or Christ). Communication is through nonverbal thoughts. Many are asked in a very nonjudgmental way, "What have you done with your life?" They may witness a visual review of their life. When they view scenes where they were unselfish and exhibited love it brought them peace. Scenes in which they might have been unkind to someone brings them sadness. Many claim they could actually feel the other person's hurt at their unkindness. However, they seemed to be judging themselves. They describe only feelings of intense joy, acceptance, and love from the light or being. These feelings then create in them a desire to give this same love to others.

Dead Relatives Appear

Many are greeted by deceased relatives and friends. One young woman promised before her death that she would greet her brother when it was his turn to die. This deceased sister kept her promise and was the first relative that came when her brother had a "Near-Death Experience" years later. She also told him he couldn't stay with her yet, and he was returned to earth with an assignment [9, p. 32].

This idea was not really new to me. I remember the day my grandmother died. I was working in the same hospital she was staying in for tests on her heart. I had come to help her eat dinner on my lunch break. She visited a little with me, yet was weak and not interested in eating much. At one point she looked off into one corner of the room and called, "Will." My grandfather William's nickname. He had been dead about ten years. I told her she must miss him very much. She died unexpectedly a few hours later.

Another time Dennis went to visit a terminally ill friend and found her logical, coherent, and relaxed. She seemed energized and peaceful about her illness and impending death. He asked her why she was this way. She responded, "Oh I wasn't going to mention it, but my mother who died some years ago visited me before you arrived." This woman also died a few days later. I believed the story when my husband shared it with me. I continued to ask myself, "Why was it now so difficult to find spiritual recovery and healing?"

I also found accounts of visitations from deceased relatives to people who were awake and not dying [10, 11]. Forty-two percent of Americans claim they've had some form of contact with a deceased person [5]. Sixty-nine percent of Americans say they believe in angels. Thirty-two percent feel they have had contact with angels [12].

Brightness, Beauty versus Dull, Gray

Many describe different scenes including beautiful gardens, bright cities of light, and bright spirit beings. Some describe people who seem to be "tied" to the earth as if in an imprisoned state, only able to go on after solving particular problems. They describe these individuals and places as gray, dull, or with a thick film dividing them from the beautiful colors and light.

Some of the individuals who were interviewed had attempted suicide, clinically died and then returned. After their near-death experience these people also were now convinced that their lives did have meaning and purpose. The problems they were trying to escape this earth from, still seemed to be there to work on after death! Yet the light was forgiving, loving, and understanding. Very few who had these experiences tried to commit suicide again. They returned and tried harder to solve their problems or at least endure them (see suicide in Chapter 9).

Many of the dying described being able to hear or feel the prayers of others. Many had no previous idea of how powerful the faith and prayers offered for them by others could be.

They Must Return

Most of the people who experience a NDE do not want to return to earth. They feel such love and joy that when they realize or are told that they must return to earth they often resist. Earth life appears so dim and gray in comparison. Yet when they do return to their bodies and to earth, almost all of them want to be kinder people. They want to give more and love others unconditionally. They desire to give the same unconditional love they had felt from the "light." They try to describe their experiences—with great difficulty. They felt they had received many answers to their questions, yet now may not even remember the questions.

A Time to Die

Some claim they were given a choice to stay. One woman explains that she was shown future events in her earth life that persuaded her to return [7, p. 117]. Although she couldn't remember details she felt she had some important work to accomplish before she should die.

> "I felt a mission, a purpose; I didn't know what it was, but I knew that my life on earth had not been meaningless." She was also told, "Your death was premature, it is not yet your time" [7, p. 42].

Could this belief comfort thousands who feel their loved one's death was an accident or mistake? Do we have a "time" to die, and if it's not the right time might we be among the thousands who have had "Near-Death Experiences" and were sent back to earth? [1, Ecclesiastes 3:2]. Consider the death of young children:

> These spirits did not need the development that would result from longer lives in mortality, and their deaths would provide challenges that would help their parents grow. The grief that comes here is intense but short. After we are united again, and only the joy of our growth and togetherness is felt [7, pp. 95, 96].

Choice or Fate?

Betty Eade felt she gained insight in her "Near-Death Experience" for those who face special challenges. The insight she shares may apply for any suffering. She felt she saw:

> One exceptionally brilliant and dynamic spirit was just entering his mother's womb. He had chosen to enter this world mentally handicapped. He was very excited about this opportunity and was aware of the growth he and his parents would achieve. The three of them had bonded with each other and planned for this arrangement long before [7, pp. 94, 95].

Could all or part of this experience be true? These feelings contrast dramatically with those expressed by the mother of a severely mentally and physically challenged child, who wrote:

I am not sure I believe in God, that for sure I do not believe these children are "planned" by any higher being. They are accidents, terrible and tragic accidents, resulting from genetic misfortune or medical incompetence, or unexplainable injury [13, p. 114].

"Where is her hope?" How can she and other parents ever gain peace? Yet some have argued that those who do not believe in a supreme being are not confused or disappointed that He failed them. They cannot feel angry with God if they do not believe He exists. Even when this mother got some control back into her life, by placing her child in a residential home, she could still not find much joy in parenting him, "No, I could never be glad to have a child like Zachy" [13, p. 237]. She loved him in a special way, yet her deep chronic sorrow for her situation never left her. Once when she thought he was dying she said, "Would that I could believe in angels, then in another time and place he could be whole and at peace" [13, p. 228].

Why couldn't she believe? Would it have brought her peace? With time I decided to interview many of the parents I worked with and found as did Ronald Knapp, that it was rare that parents could totally resolve the death of their children without some hope or belief that they exist somewhere, most have hope and faith they will see them again [14, p. 36].

CHILDREN AND NEAR-DEATH EXPERIENCE

Some of the most interesting experiences reported are from children. Dr. Melvin Morse in his book, *Closer to the Light,* addresses children's reports [15]. Some children have reported seeing a relative or would call out a relative's name who had died. Many have talked of "angels singing." I remember another account where a dying child told his mother that a deceased aunt had come to take him with her. He died soon after. Some other children who had attempted suicide because they were abused or felt no one cared for them were told they could be kind and nurturing to themselves, and "to stick around and see what you can do with your life" [15, pp. 159-161; 16, p. 258].

Would young children lie or make up these stories? Why did their stories have the same elements as the adult NDEs? Their simple innocent accounts were ringing truth to my ears. Was my heart, mind, and soul regaining peace and understanding?

I really wanted to have my own NDE, or a visitation! However, reading the accounts of others helped me validate my own unique experiences. These include death preparations, impressions, dreams, and visions. We will share some of these in this chapter.

DEATH PREPARATIONS

Death preparations are different than NDEs. They come in many forms. Events, feelings, forebodings, dreams, visions, and impressions can all be death preparations.

I learned that many children talk about death or have death preparations before they actually die [15]. Some are children who know they will die soon from their terminal illness and some are healthy children who die suddenly and unexpectedly.

I reviewed my journal a year or so before Cam's death and found many elements of death preparations. I read events I had written many years ago and realized how often Cameron talked about death, and about his "Next Life."

When he was eight years old I recorded in my journal on two different occasions where he requested to go to "Heaven." He said, "I want to go visit God and become "whole." I don't recall using the term "whole" with him and I wrote, "I hope he's kidding because I would be lost without him!"

At age thirteen Dennis asked him on video, "Does it make you feel bad that you can't walk?" He responded, "No, you get used to it." His dad then asked, "Do you think you'll ever walk?" He replied, "Up in Heaven." His dad pushed him more and said, "Well, are you excited about going to Heaven?!" "Yea!" he said. "When do you think you are going there?" He giggled and said, "Today!" Then he giggled some more and said he was teasing us about the date! He continued this kind of talk up until his death. He wrote a poem for the school's cultural arts contest. This was six months before his death:

If I Had A Wish

If I had a wish I would wish that I could walk!
I would run and play and all the girls would like me.
See it's hard to be different in some ways.
Like you can't do your homework without someone helping you.
Sports would be fun to do, and I would play basketball.
And I wouldn't miss standing in my prone stander if I could walk.
In some ways not walking is good luck because you get to drive
   early!
(My wheelchair) And you don't even have to have a license.

> You also can have a computer all to yourself.
> My wish will come true—in the next Life!

He seemed to balance the realities of his hardships with the positive aspects of his life. I admired his attitude, "Yea, sometimes it's hard, but I am still happy."

Parents of disabled, chronically and terminally ill children are often worried for their child's safety. They often ask, "How can I protect my weak child?" I too had this worry. I often feared Cam would die from an accident. He was always falling off his trike and even with his helmet on, seemed vulnerable at all times. I wrote about one particular injury that I felt responsible for.

> Today I unhooked Cam from his prone standing table to carry him into the bathroom. His brother came running into the room carrying his little sister who had just smashed her finger in the door. As I turned to see how much she was bleeding, Cameron fell out of the stander and hit the right side of his head on our tiled fireplace. I turned him over and he had a very blank stare on his face. Fear gripped me as I thought, "I have killed my son, or that he could have serious head injuries." When he became alert he was pale and shaking. He did recover. I cried off and on all day. I feared he might die young and possibly from a serious accident that I could have prevented. How can I protect him? I don't want to live my life without him. I prayed that God would help me protect him, and grant me the privilege of caring for him a long time.

I then promised myself we were going to make the most of our time. I felt we had done this in the past, but now I was even more determined. (This was 15 months before his death.)

MAKING THE MOST NOW

I would think of things he had never experienced and try to make the most of life! For spring break we drove a long distance to the beach. Although he had been to beaches, he had never tried surfing! It was as much work for us to keep him lying on the board as it was for him. He laughed and was so proud. Later we camped, and he was thrilled to feed some sea gulls right out of his hands from his wheelchair.

When summer came we drove the 1300 miles to see grandparents and cousins. We took him to the zoo again, and spent two days in his favorite amusement park.

With fall and school upon us, it was hectic! However, we had a wonderful Thanksgiving weekend together, and again went "home" for Christmas. These trips were thrilling to Cam. He loved to travel, eat out, and swim in the motel's pool. He loved to see his grandparents, aunts, uncles, cousins, and his friend Doug, all people he loved and who helped him feel his own self-worth.

When spring came we found ourselves again camping and flying kites together. After church on Easter Sunday, Cam rode his adapted bike while we walked to the duck pond near our home. We felt such family unity and joy. I honestly wondered if life could get much better than this.

In April we took him on another trip where his dad had to work. We showed him a new lake and campground, he especially enjoyed riding in a big ski tube pulled behind the boat. We are glad we spent so much time together that year enjoying his company, because in May he was gone!

As we reviewed many of our experiences with Cameron we felt they helped us prepare for his death. The events also helped us accept his painful parting and our grief a little easier. We are grateful and cherish these sweet memories of our lives together.

BEFORE DEATH DREAMS

Dreams are a series of ideas, emotions, or images occurring during sleep stages. Most of us dream one and a half hours each night, even though we may not remember what we dream [17, p. 72].

In my research I learned that dreams can have elements from our past, present, and sometimes our future. They may bring us insight or be insignificant. The Bible has many accounts of individuals being guided by their or other's dreams. The most familiar account is where Joseph is warned in a dream to flee from King Herod with Mary and baby Jesus [1, Matthew 2:13].

I have come to understand how dreams can prepare people for upcoming death. I've read a few written accounts of people's dreams before their loved one's death. I also talked with a mother who dreamed she and her seven year old were in a large crowd and became separated. She became very emotional and woke up crying because she had actually allowed him to go and didn't try to find him. The dream left her distraught and concerned. Her son had also recently asked her what it was like to die. She remembers telling him that someone he knew would meet him. This was a healthy child who suddenly became ill and died twenty-four hours later. Before he died his mother thought she heard the words, "Mommy, please stop calling me back, I want to live with Jesus." She then realized, "I had been willing him in my mind to fight and come back to me." Her husband had been lying by him and although the life support seemed to still be working, he felt his soul had left his body. As he was meditating about how he would deal with his son's death he felt he saw him in the hospital hall with a deceased great grandfather. Soon after the doctors told these parents that although he appeared to be alive with life support, there was no brain activity left.

When my grandfather died, my mother (his daughter) was only fourteen. She recalls waking up from a very real dream about his death. She cried and mourned, however, later that morning when she was told he actually had died, she felt somehow better prepared by the dream.

I didn't remember my mother's dream until long after I experienced my own dream about Cameron's death.

> One week before Cam's surgery I dreamed his surgery was over and the doctors said they needed to talk to me. They told me he was having trouble breathing and would have to be on "life support," and that he would not be able to live without it. Of course they recommended the machines be removed. However, it was my decision.
>
> I went into his room and watched the cardiac monitor move with each thump of his heart. I knew if I told them to turn off the ventilator (breathing machine) the line on the heart monitor would soon go in a straight line instead of up and down (death). I thought about it for a long time. Finally I ran out of the room crying. I realized I could not tell them to unplug my child's life! I wanted him alive!

The dream was so real I woke up sobbing. I have never felt so afraid or sad after a dream! I shared my dream with my mother and later called my husband. He related similar feelings that had caused him to worry about Cameron also. After his death our guilt pushed us to ask ourselves, "Why didn't we cancel the surgery?!" "Was this a warning?" However with time, we chose to believe the dream was a glimpse into the future to help prepare us for his death?

The night before his surgery I shared my dream with Cam. I didn't want to frighten him, I just wanted him to know how much I loved him and how hard it would be to live without him if something went wrong. I also told him if something did go wrong and he really died, would he please try to somehow let me know he was well and happy. He nodded yes, yet as I looked at those big brown eyes I realized that would be a huge promise to keep. I then said, "If he couldn't return and tell me (visitation), I would try to just have faith to know he was okay." He again agreed like so many times before when I made a request of him. Although we had this frank discussion, I don't think any of us really believed it could happen to us! I honestly did not remember the dream until several days after his death and my mother brought it up. In a unique way it became an important event that helped to bring us comfort and accept his death.

VISIONS

Some feel it is hard to tell the difference between a dream and a vision. Others say a vision is so real, you are awake and see what is happening, where in dreams you know you are sleeping. Visions may occur in the day or at night. The Bible mentions "night visions" [1, Daniel 2:19].

I remember my mother telling me how sad her own mother was when her husband died. Six months later she followed him to the grave. Although it was hard on my mother to lose both her parents so close together as a fourteen-year-old girl, she felt some happiness because she believed her mother was relieved of her grief and was now with her husband. One of her brothers said later he actually saw these parents happily together in a vision. This brought peace and comfort to the ten children they had left behind.

The day Cameron died, his Special Education teacher, Janice Willis remembered the poem he had written earlier about his wishes. She had trouble sleeping and early that morning had the following experience. She got up and put her impressions to prose: She wrote "Written in response to the death of Cameron Ashton and his private wish for his Next Life."

THE WISH

I felt the breath of death today. It brushed against my cheek. And left me most unconscious, taking thought and words to speak. It left me feeling empty, and lost within myself. It crept about my being like a mouse on pantry shelf. I wandered aimless through the day and half the lonely night, but came a "Great Awakening" at break of morning light, I saw a child in field of green with yellow flowers round. He was moving swiftly through the grass on limbs so strong and sound. His laughter rang within my ear as clear as Sunday's bell. His smile did light the broad blue sky and caused the clouds to swell. I watched as one who's privileged eyes had glimpsed through Heavens door, and just as quickly saw it close, revealing nothing more. Then as a wave upon a shore, washes it so clean. My torched mind was cleared to see that this was not a dream. The sorrow felt inside my heart belonged to only me. For how could I be sad for one who's now so free? I swept away a tear that trickled down my cheek. And rose to meet the bright new day that God had given me. I felt witness to a sacred time, not really meant to me. For how often does God grant a wish and allow someone to see!?

We didn't know her well and she was hesitant to share her experience with us. It wasn't until after the funeral she went home and brought us the poem. Several weeks later after we asked for more details, she acknowledged it was more than a dream. She felt it was a vision and did not understand why it happened to her. She did say that she had never been touched spiritually so profoundly by any other student during her fifteen years of teaching. Her poem has brought comfort and peace to our hearts.

I have read and talked with people who feel they have had a vision about an upcoming event that occurs or have viewed someone who has died. Many times it is years after the death occurs.

The most impressive visions I read about happen at the moment of death. The deceased are viewed by a loved one who is not only unaware of the event, but is many miles from its occurrence. Joseph Heinerman in his book, *Spirit World Manifestations,* tells a story of a man who left his home in the states to work several months in London.

One morning he found himself visiting his home back in the states. His wife was sitting back in her rocking chair with her eyes closed. He went toward her to inquire as to how she was and reached out to touch her. He was shocked to discover her skin was cold and she was dead. He kept telling himself this is not a dream, this is really happening! It wasn't until several days later that he got word of how they found his wife dead in her rocking chair! [10, p. 175].

VISITATIONS

A visitation is the act of being visited. Although many visitations seem to occur as dreams, I read some accounts occurring while the person was awake and it occurred during daylight hours.

One such visitation occurred to a woman at her sewing machine. Her mother who had been dead sometime, came with an important message for her. She said, "Daughter, you don't know what it has cost me to come to you" [10, p. 84]. Another similar account said, "You are the only one I have to depend. . . . Don't fail in this" [10, p. 86].

One day in my husband's counseling session, a widower described in detail a visit from his deceased wife. It concerned him very much because she had encouraged him to marry a certain woman he knew to help take care of their children. He wasn't really sure he was ready to marry, or wanted to marry this person! In 1993 approximately 66 percent of widows experience apparitions after their husbands die [5].

Another experience that was comforting was when a deceased mother appeared to her grieving daughter and said, "I was allowed to come and tell you not to be worried about me. I don't suffer anymore and I am very happy" [11, p. 44]. (She died from cancer.) She made it clear that she had to have permission to come. There is also an account of a man's wife visiting him eighteen years after her death [11, p. 65].

An interesting account happened in Cokeville, Wyoming in 1986. Some children describe how they were warned about a bomb that was about to go off in their school. They claim some people dressed in white standing in the air above them told them where to go and what to do. There was more than one account and all the children lived after the bomb exploded to tell their story [18].

After the event the children were shown pictures of dead relatives they hadn't known. Some they recognized as the people in white who helped them.

It seems that some departed loved ones may be allowed to return to offer comfort, warn, or give an important message. In 1993, 75 percent of parents who have lost children claim they have had some apparition with that child [5]. Yet, in many near-death accounts, those dying have asked to communicate with the living and are told they cannot.

At first I really felt my son would return and give me a message. Because this expectation did not occur, I believe it contributed to my spiritual injury. However, as time went on I decided to take a positive view, either he couldn't, or as described earlier, it would "cost" him too much. I also chose to believe, "Blessed are they that have not seen, and yet have believed" [1, John 20:29].

One day as I was feeling sad and down (it had been close to 2 years since his death), I cried out in prayer, "how long will it hurt so much? The pain keeps coming back! I missed him so much." Then I heard a silent voice in my heart and mind tell me to read the Bible. I turned to Jeremiah 31, "A strange place to read," I thought. I'm not sure I had read here before. When I got to verse 15-17 my heart leaped.

I felt the Lord was trying to comfort me, and all those who have ever or will ever lose a child!

> Thus saith the Lord; A voice was heard in Ramah, lamentation and bitter weeping; Rahel weeping for her children refused to be comforted for her children, because they were not. Thus saith the Lord; Refrain thy voice from weeping, and thine eyes from tears: for thy work shall be rewarded, saith the Lord; and they shall come again. . . . And there is hope in thine end saith the Lord, that thy children shall come again . . . [1].

It hit me with great force and power. I learned later this counsel was to be for the mothers mourning for their children King Herod had ordered killed [1, Matthew 3:17-18]. These inspired words have given me more faith and strength to endure the wait!

IMPRESSIONS

Impressions come to many people in all facets of life. These impressions differ from opinions. They are strong feelings that Webster's dictionary defines as stamped deeply in the mind. A fixed mark causing psychological effect or influence. Some may feel intuitions, premonitions, or revelations are similar to impressions. Impressions can bring us worry, comfort, or help us make a decision. Some people claim they knew something was going to occur before it actually did, due to an impression. One mother of a cystic fibrosis child wrote,

> The day after we were diagnosed, the doctor at the Children's Hospital wanted to do the same test on my older son. He is asthmatic and small so he fit the cystic fibrosis category. I had felt that God had dumped me on the ground when the test came back positive. I prayed and cried and screamed for hours. I felt very alone even in the arms of my husband. Finally . . . in the shower at 3 A.M. I had the most calming feeling I have ever had. It was as though I had come to a definite decision. . . . Brandon's next test would be negative, a 32. (Which is a normal score.) That day came to pass. The medical professional wanted to do another test to be sure. I again had this overwhelming feeling it would be negative for cystic fibrosis, and a score of 28. That too became true! Only then did I realize that God had not left me in the cold and dark, he was by my side and if I let him, he will help me through this. I remember my mother saying, "God never gives us more than we can handle." Though sometimes it doesn't seem that way, and I am

not a religious person, we just may not know our limits as well as He does.

The scripture actually says God will not give us more TEMPTA-TION than we can bear, without HELPING us find a way to escape [1, I Corinthians 10:13]. We discourage people from using these kinds of cliches. It can hurt people spiritually who have had a loved one commit suicide when they didn't feel they could cope with their situation. Also telling people their loved one died because God took, needed, or wanted them. Some mothers feel God already has lots of babies, and they only had one! This can cause confusion and anger toward God. The unsaid or hidden message conveys that God may have his fingers on gun triggers, steering wheels, or in other ways that causes accidents. It seems to cause less spiritual injury if one can assume God allowed us to come to an imperfect world where natural disasters and accidents occur. Remember, He is there to comfort us, and help us through it.

Cameron seemed to have his own impressions and death preparations. I feel the following quote from a video suggests that Cameron knew all along what death was and what it would bring. When his dad was filming him he had the impression that what Cameron was saying was deeply significant, more than the typical family video session. This was six weeks before his death. Among other things, Cameron stated,

> . . . I really feel that I can walk in the next life, and that I can talk better. And that I live forever in the next life after this and that I will see God again. And I get to see my grandma and grandpa who died a couple years ago, again. And you can too someday. I guess I don't have to say anymore. And this is Cameron signing off.

We were nervous when the funeral home called and asked if we wanted to view Cameron's body before the services. At first my husband thought he might just drive me over and wait in the car. When we arrived he decided to come in with me. We couldn't believe our eyes! There lying in the casket was not the same helpless child we had cared for, for over fourteen years. We saw and felt impressed, "Here lies a strong valiant young man!" Instead of looking nine or ten years old, he looked eighteen or nineteen years old! We had never seen his face and hands straight and relaxed due to the spasms and tight muscles from cerebral palsy. He looked so handsome and tall now in his dark suit and red tie. Our fears about viewing him disappeared and we sat basking in the peace and comfort we were feeling. Did Cameron get his "Wish?"

Was he free from his cerebral palsy, on a new mission, experiencing his "next life?"

My sister and mother also spoke of several impressions they had while they were alone with Cameron's body. They felt, "That he had passed or completed his early mission and test, that there was purpose in his life and his death, and all his earthly challenges were now gone."

Before Cameron's surgery, Dennis said a special prayer (blessing) for Cameron. He felt "impressed" Cameron would be going on some sort of "mission." (This was confusing to him because of Cam's young age and limitations.) He wrote,

> I was hesitant to verbalize that impression until later. My wife and I took the opportunity to talk to Cameron about his future, God's love, and the possibility of his death. Looking back we can note about sixteen impressions and death preparations. This helped two committed parents prepare for a future event that would test their very being.

Another person who had feelings and put them into writing was one of Cam's uncles. He described his "impressions" at the funeral. Dennis was feeling grief and great guilt that maybe he could have somehow saved his son's life. This account of another's impressions brought hope and comfort to his troubled mind.

> Dennis told me of how he had waited by Cam's hospital bed in the early hours of the morning until Cam was finally asleep and how he then fell asleep himself only to awaken twenty or so minutes later and find that Cam had passed away. When I heard this I remembered the story about a young boy that lived by us when I was growing up. He developed leukemia when he was ten or eleven years old. For the next year or so, he and his parents spent many days in and out of hospitals. There were times when things looked hopeful, but in the end the disease was winning the fight and when the final curtains came to a close on his life, he and his parents found themselves alone in a hospital room once again. They were talking quietly together when he looked up and started to talk to someone. When his father asked him who he was talking to, he said, "Can't you see him? Jesus is here. He's come to get me." He started to get out of bed and then laid back and closed his eyes for the last time.

> Could it be that night in the hospital, the heavens knew it was Cam's time to return home? And doesn't it make sense that for

someone as pure in heart as Cameron, this homecoming would be one of peace and joy? Isn't it possible that heavenly messengers were standing in the wings as Dennis spent his last few quiet moments with Cameron, waiting there for Dennis to peacefully fall asleep. Doesn't it seem perfect that at that moment, Cameron would arise in a radiant light, not as a weak crippled boy, but as a tall, stately young man, experiencing once again the freedom of movement that he hadn't felt since his mortal birth. And although it would be tempting to pursue this new freedom and immediately return to Heavenly father's presence, the picture that came to my mind was Cameron walking over to his father and lovingly placing a hand on his head, perhaps in deep gratitude for all the sacrifice that he and his family had made in his behalf, or perhaps as a gesture of comfort knowing of the pain and sorrow that would soon come. Although it may not have happened exactly as it came to my mind, I believe with all my heart that Cam's passing was one of peace and joy.

A friend and neighbor brought us a large wrapped gift the day after Cameron died. As soon as I opened the gift I felt the impact and power of this gift. It was a beautiful picture of Christ healing the blind man. Our family, and especially Cameron, loved the stories about Christ's healings [1, Matthew 11:5, 15:31, and John 9:1-10]. The following story describes several impressions she had that led to the picture that now hangs in our home [19, pp. 47-49].

She was a young mother who wanted to buy some art to hang in her home where her children could view and appreciate spiritual things. She had a particular picture in mind and had bought it with some other items when she found herself being drawn to the picture of Christ healing a blind man. She put it back, reasoning that she had enough and her time and money were spent! As she walked away she wrote that she felt,

> a nagging, rather irritable feeling. The feeling dragged at me until I turned back and added the picture of the miracle to my purchases. I would frame the others, I reasoned. This one I would just take out and look at now and again.

She didn't understand why this picture had created such a strong impression. Later, she wondered if she was drawn to the picture because she had a disabled sister, or she wondered if the child she was then carrying might not be normal? She had a frame and beautiful matt selected for the original picture she had planned to frame, yet she wrote,

It looked all wrong. I tried other pictures I had planned to frame with the same result. Finally I lifted the picture of the Christ healing the blind man from the box and placed it in the frame. An overwhelming spirit filled the room. It looked lovely. It fit. I turned the picture over and read the description on the back. "And his disciples asked him, saying, Master, who did sin, this man, or his parents, that he was born blind?" Jesus answered, "Neither hath this blind man sinned, nor his parents: but that the works of God should be made manifest in him" [1, John 9:3]. I never understood this. Jesus healed him and so the works of God were manifest, but what about all those who are not healed? What about my handicapped sister who had died when I was a child? What about Cameron Ashton . . . confined to a wheelchair? Suddenly my mind flooded with strong, almost overwhelming impressions. I began to see very clearly. I understood many things I had not understood before. At one point I thought clearly, "I am being taught by the spirit." . . . I see Cameron, my sister, others I have known. They are "challenged" in mind or body. Others carry them. They are their arms, their legs, their minds. I see these same individuals giving to the weak in spirit. I see their gifts of love and hope. I see the works of God made manifest for them and by them. I sat down weakly on the bed. Why is this happening to me?

The day she heard Cameron, who attended school with her sons, was having surgery, she felt the impression, "Cameron is not long for this world." She clapped her hands over her ears. "What a morbid thought," she said out loud! She then dismissed it, "Not long for this world could mean five or six years!"

A couple of days after Cam's surgery, a friend of hers called by mistake, meaning to call someone else. She told her Cameron Ashton had died and then apologized for her mistaken call. Stunned by the news, she said, "I don't think it was a mistake, thanks for calling!" She then knew why she was so drawn to the beautiful picture on her wall. She took it down and wrapped it up. She worried about what we would think when she walked into our grief with such a gift. Then this message came to her, and she wrote, "The Lord loves you, and I, more than we can comprehend. He wants you to know this was meant to be. He wants you to be comforted. He wants you to remember how His works were manifest in your son's life, and in your lives because of that son." She felt the spirit had helped her gain understanding of the picture. She felt Cameron had manifested the works of God in many ways during his short life. She shared the ways he had touched their family, and her impressions that he was now healed, and doing other important work.

These spiritual impressions shared by others have been another source of comfort and spiritual healing to us.

MY OWN IMPRESSIONS

Soon after Cameron's death I was walking through the same "sand hills" I often had escaped to as a teenager. I was crying, praying, and mourning, "Why Me!" I then had some thoughts and impressions. They may have been simple logical thoughts that anyone could have said to me. However, when they came into my mind and heart I felt the truth of these words with force. I heard in my soul and heart two things, "Cameron did exist and was doing something important," also that as dark and dreary as this earth looked to me now, "I too still had a purpose or mission that needed to be completed." I made the decision to try, not knowing then how hard it would be.

Three months after his death, Dennis and I performed a special ordinance (religious rite) in Cameron's behalf. The men sat on one side of the room and the women on the other. It was a very small company and so there was only one row of women and two rows of men. Cam's dad sat on the second row of the men's side. I kept feeling like someone was sitting behind me. I looked and the whole back of the room was empty. The feeling became so intense that I came to feel Cameron must be behind me! I couldn't see him, I just felt his presence. It was confusing to me, because I thought, "If he could come and watch this ceremony for himself, why would he sit on the women's side?" Was it just my imagination, or wishful thinking? After the ceremony, I asked Dennis if he thought it was possible for Cameron's spirit to really be there. He said, "I think so, and he was sitting right beyond you!" This confirmed my impression and brought us more comfort.

AFTER DEATH DREAMS

As stated earlier everyone dreams about ninety minutes a night [17, p. 72]. In early grief, some parents have reported having nightmares and insomnia. Later, many parents desire to dream about their deceased child. Some have profound dreams about their child and others never dream of their child at all. Research is not clear as to why. Mary Edmonds, an MSW counselor, says dreams can offer comfort to parents. She recommends if someone is desiring a dream, that before they fall asleep they should spend some time thinking and meditating about the deceased. This meditation may help them have a dream about their loved one. In her research she has found dreams often offer comfort. They do not generally have any negative effects.

Soon after Cameron died, one of my brothers and a good friend each shared a dream they had. Both of their dreams had to do with Cameron and water. In my brother's dream, Cameron was drowning and my brother was trying to help Dennis keep his head above the water. In Pam's dream her son was drowning and she understood he would be going to "Heaven" to be with Cameron. Both of these people described feeling extremely anxious and distraught. They felt they got a glimpse of the pain and loss of control we were feeling. They were then able to understand more fully and comfort us.

I have had a few dreams about Cameron. Some have been very real and have brought a sense of spiritual healing.

> In one dream I was intensely crying and missing Cameron. I was told in my dream to get up and read the words to a song called "Come Unto Jesus." I woke myself up and went to find the book which the song was in. The words that finally brought peace and comfort were, "Oh know ye not that angels are near you from brightest mansions above?"

Did I know? Was I regaining my faith, hope, and knowledge?

The night before Easter I was reading about the resurrection. Cameron had been gone about one year. I had experienced a couple of dreams about him that year and they were usually about me caring for him again as a young child. This Easter morning I woke up early from a wonderful dream, yet it felt different than a dream, I like to think of it as a vision.

> Cameron was walking toward me. He had a beautiful smile on his face. He looked older (like he had looked in the casket) and my impression was that it was the resurrection and we were joining each other. I didn't get to talk to him, or hug him, yet the joy I felt was beyond description. It was the most peaceful, joyous feeling I have ever experienced. If I live to a hundred years old I hope I will never forget that peace.

Rabindranath Tagore said,

> Death is not extinguishing the light; it is putting out the lamp because the dawn has come [8, p. 12].

OUR OWN NEAR-DEATH EXPERIENCE

After all this research and reading about "near-death experiences," I really wanted my own! I thought since Cameron hasn't been able to come back to me and let me know he's okay, I could go to him! I did have some surgery, however I had no "Near-Death Experience," just pain!

A few months after Cam's death I felt pressed to call a friend and neighbor the night before his open heart surgery. It was embarrassing to request such a strange thing. I tried to explain that I knew his surgery was very serious and maybe he would have a "near-death experience." I told him I didn't think or hope he was going to die! However, if he did, to check on Cameron and give him my love! Gordon was very kind and said he would try to fulfill my request if such an event occurred. He returned home in good health and did not have a near-death experience.

Then an unusual thing happened. Gordon had been home several days when he developed complications and had to go back to the hospital for an emergency gallbladder removal. He was very weakened by the first surgery and had to receive blood before he could have this second surgery. They feared he would not last long enough to even receive the needed blood. Fortunately he did. After the surgery the doctors told him he had gone into congestive heart failure. He recalls being awake during the surgery and hearing the doctors and nurses concern as they hurried about to resuscitate his heart. He felt himself being led to a large room full of many deceased persons. He saw Cameron among them. He was walking and talking with another young man. He appeared happy, busy, and apparently had important work to do. Gordon desired to go to him and speak with him, yet was restrained and led back to earth where he woke up in the intensive care unit. Although he was too ill to tell us his story until many days later, he sent his wife immediately to briefly explain his experience. He now also feels Cameron got his wish!

His experience was almost like a personal "Near-Death Experience" for me! It has been a comfort to reflect on his NDE and feel I got a quick glimpse of Cameron in his "Next Life!"

How grateful we are for the many people that have come to us and shared their love, impressions, and spiritual experiences. My spiritual healing was progressing, however, my studying continued! I wanted to combine all this knowledge . . . of mind, body, soul.

MIND–BODY–SOUL

I found recovery can be enhanced by "Sharpening the Saw" in our personal lives through regular exercise of mind, body, and soul [20, p. 47]. Surrounding ourselves with as much "good" as possible in each of these three areas can bring healing. Our study, meditation, and healthy thought processes, blended with sound psychology can build correct thinking (healthy minds). Reading, crying, talking, and writing can help release our pain and build emotional security. This active participation can build our self-esteem and bring us understanding of our grief. Physical exercise, eating, and sleeping properly helps us improve and maintain healthy minds and bodies. Building and strengthening our faith, like our muscles requires time, education, and hard work. Belief may be passive, however, faith is active. Current studies show faith is a strong indicator for helping people cope and enjoy a worthwhile and satisfying life. I found, in my research, a strong link between faith and physical health as well as mental health. Clergymen have enjoyed a longer life span than other professionals. Church attenders in some studies have lower blood pressure, leave the hospital earlier, and ward off illness and depression better than those not interested in religion.

An article in the *USA Today* described how more of the half-million physical scientists in the United States are discussing religion, which at one time was an unspoken taboo. They identify physicians who are connecting mind, body, and soul in the healing process. Many are exploring the complex nature of the universe, and questioning their original theories that it all came about by chance [21].

The new DSM IV (a diagnostic guide for psychiatrists, psychologists, and professional psychotherapists) now has a religious or spiritual problems section for diagnosing clients who have had distressing spiritual experiences [22, p. 812]. The DSM III did not have this section, so unfortunately many previous clients who experienced personal spiritual problems may have been labeled as "neurotic" or even "psychotic" [23].

PSYCHOLOGY AND SPIRITUALITY

Many therapists in the western world now seem to accept and deal with spirituality as a part of their psychotherapy. Individuals discovered, through study and meditation, how to gain not only a sense of who they are, but also came to understand how they fit into our universe with God. This walk with faith or journey may increase self-awareness as they look inward, rather than outward for answers. Some may call this experience being "born-again." I agree with those who call it . . . "Re-cognitions" an idea that suggests we are "knowing again" something that we knew before, something that has lain hidden from us while we sought knowledge in the outer world" [24, p. 279]. This could be called revelations, or gaining insights and truth. "And this is life eternal, that they might know thee the only true God, and Jesus Christ, whom thou hast sent" [1, John 17:3].

As part of earth life we all will feel varying degrees of pain as we experience trials and adversity. In the past, many have tried to rely solely on one of the following: professional therapy, self-help, or religion. As mentioned previously, you may require all of these tools to heal. "Ye shall know the truth, and the truth shall make you free" [1, John 8:32]. We can become free from our pain through learning and combining all true principles. These may include professional or scientific knowledge, understanding of grief theory, and learning how to apply other true principles, like the power of faith.

I feel Dennis explained it well in an article he wrote for work entitled "Religious Views Relative to Professional Therapy":

> Prior to development of the professional practice of psychotherapy, issues currently dealt with by professional counselors, were more often handled by Religious Leaders. Difficulties such as grieving, marital discord, depression, etc., were once handled almost exclusively by Religious Leaders. With the emerging field of psychotherapy, increasing numbers of individuals suffering from life's challenges have sought professional psychotherapists. Some of these individuals have been drawn away from their ecclesiastical leaders and their more typical biblical solutions. Others have remained, strongly anchored to their religious faith, unwilling to acknowledge any validity associated with the emerging science of professional psychotherapy. They have considered it a lack of faith to seek therapeutic intervention beyond that which was provided to them through the doctrinal teachings of their religious faith and their spiritual leaders. Some have felt more comfortable putting their faith in God rather than in psychological research and science. Unfortunately, this tendency has been enhanced by some professional therapists who universally challenge any client's reliance or comfort that is derived through compliance to traditional religious teachings, doctrines, or counsel. Some therapists would go so far as to label any client adherence to a religious framework for dealing with life's problems as neurotic behavior at best.

Those of us who maintain allegiance to gospel principles, as well as expertise in the emerging social sciences, should strive to reduce the tension between religion and professional psychotherapy. This can be done by developing therapy modalities that are based on gospel principles and practiced in a moral based environment. We must also strive to educate both those within our profession who quickly discount the significance of personal religious experience, as well as those outside our profession who espouse an exclusive religious orientation to solve all emotional and psychological challenges.

Undefiled religion encompasses and utilizes all truth, including that which has emerged from the fields of psychotherapy and social work. These truths, when properly utilized in psychotherapy, not only originate from the same source, but have the same redeeming results for clients who appropriately apply these correct principles in their lives [25].

We were finding our healing enhanced through both the spiritual realm and sound psychology. Exercising our spirit through daily prayer, study, meditation, and service to others helped us develop a firm faith and knowledge concerning our purpose here on earth and confirmed our destination hereafter.

THE FINAL POWER

I recall years ago a peace came to my soul when the following Bible scriptures were mailed to me by my father when he knew I was struggling to accept Cameron's diagnosis. I had heard them before, however, in my sorrow they meant more. I feel they have continued to help me overcome many of life's challenges. ". . . We glory in tribulations knowing that tribulations worketh patience; and patience experience; and experience, hope" [1, Romans 5:3, 4). "For I reckon that the sufferings of this present time are not worthy to be compared with the glory which shall be revealed in us" [1, Romans 8:18]. ". . . nothing can separate us from the love of Christ" [1, Romans 8:35-39]. "But he knoweth the way that I take: when he hath tried me, I shall come forth as gold" [1, Job 23:10].

Adversity can teach us things we can learn in no other way. It can make us learn, stretch, and grow, even when we don't want to! When we feel we have nothing to hold on to, faith can carry us through those darkest hours. Maybe we can learn to grieve patiently [1, 1 Peter 2:19-20]. God promises to "comforteth us in all our tribulation" [1, 2 Corinthians 1:4-7].

I believe God loves us and wants us to be happy, secure, and succeed. He allows us to experience joy and pain. He is acquainted with grief [1, Isaiah 53:3-5]. I feel he can comfort and guide us if we let him and let our faith grow just as that tiny mustard seed does. We can plant the seed by simply DESIRING faith. We can water our seed of faith by letting go of things we cannot control and by believing and trusting in a higher source to bring ultimate peace and comfort. We can nourish our faith as it sprouts and grows by praying and asking for the POWER of faith to bless our lives. We can prune by studying God's word and understanding the comfort of the atonement and resurrection. We can then harvest the peace and recover by knowing God has great power to heal and free us. He does not punish us for our mistakes by taking innocent children from us. He loves us and sacrificed his own son that we might live again.

I miss my son with all my heart. I mourn for other parents who must walk this earth without children they grew to love and adore. Study and knowledge helped me accept and understand death and grief. Yet, my true peace and comfort came through my walk to find spiritual healing. This POWER of faith and the still small voice has spoke to my heart and soul as it did to Henry Wadsworth Longfellow:

Life is real! Life is earnest! And the grave is not its goal; Dust thou art, to dust returnest, was not spoken of the soul.

I have hurt and grown. I will never be the same again. I know now all life is of great value and importance. I know more fully that we all have purpose and meaning on earth and in our "Next LIfe"! As Christ (who also wept) said to Martha, mourning for her brother, Lazarus

I am the resurrection, and the life: he that believeth in me, though he were dead, yet shall he live: And whosoever liveth and believeth in me SHALL NEVER DIE [1, John 11:25-26].

I look forward with great anticipation when I remember my dream about Cameron and the resurrection. "Because I live, ye shall live also" [1, John 14:19]. Of all the principles that have helped me heal, knowing I will meet my son again through FAITH, and the atonement brings me my greatest comfort; a comfort beyond description!

REFERENCES

1. Authorized King James version, BIBLE, A. J. Holman Co., Philadelphia.

2. M. Dickson, *Grief Recovery Seminars,* Dallas, Texas, 1991.
3. D. Edwards, *GRIEVING: The Pain and the Promise,* Covenant, Inc., Salt Lake City, Utah, 1989.
4. H. Schiff, *Living Through Mourning,* Viking Penguin Inc., New York, 1986.
5. Research collected for Oprah Winfrey, October 8, 1993.
6. R. A. Moody, *Reflections on Life after Life,* Bantam Books, New York, Introduction, 1977.
7. B. J. Eadie, *Embraced by the Light, Gold Leaf Press,* Placerville, California, 1992.
8. P. H. Dunn, *The Birth We Call Death,* Bookcraft Inc., Salt Lake City, Utah, 1976.
9. L. Nelson, *Beyond the Veil,* Vol. II, Cedar Fort, Inc., 1989.
10. J. Heinerman, *Spirit World Manifestations,* Joseph Lyon & Asso. dba Magazine Printing & Publishing, Salt Lake City, Utah, 1978.
11. M. R. Sorenson and D. R. Willmore, *The Journey Beyond Life,* Vol. I, Sounds of Zion, Inc., Midvale, Utah, 1988.
12. Time Life Video, *ANGELS,* Alexandria, Virginia, 1994.
13. F. Kupfer, *Before and After Zachariah,* Delacorte Press, New York, 1971.
14. R. L. Knapp, *Beyond Endurance,* Schocken Books, New York, 1986.
15. M. Morse, *Closer to the Light,* Villard Books, New York, 1990.
16. B. L. Top and W. C. Top, *Beyond Death's Door,* Bookcraft, Salt Lake City, Utah, 1993.
17. E. Linn, *Premonitions, Visitations and Dreams . . . of the Bereaved,* Publishers Mark, Incline Village, Nevada, 1991.
18. *Trial by Terror,* Wixom; *LA Times,* May 16-18, 1986; *School Administrator Magazine, 48,* pp. 12-17, May & June 1991; *CBS Broadcast,* 4/5/94 Save the Children.
19. *The Ensign Magazine,* Salt Lake City, Utah, September 1994.
20. S. R. Covey, *Principle-Centered Leadership,* Summit Books, New York, 1990.
21. *USA Today,* cover story of section D, March 24, 1994.
22. DSM-IV, *Diagnostic and Statistical Manual of Mental Disorders* (4th Edition), American Psychiatric Association, Washington, D.C., 1994.
23. DSM-III, *Diagnostic and Statistical Manual of Mental Disorders* (3rd Edition), American Psychiatric Association, Washington, D.C., 1987.
24. J. Rosenberg, M. Rand, and D. Asay, *Body, Self, and Soul,* Humanics New Age, Atlanta, Georgia, 1985.
25. D. Ashton, *Religious Views Relative to Professional Therapy,* unpublished paper, 1993.

CHAPTER 9

Other Considerations

EDUCATION

Disabled, chronically, and terminally ill children may receive their education in a variety of ways. Some are taken from their homes and live in state-sponsored institutions. There are also special or segregated schools where special needs children are bused to locations within a community. The most common form of education is a segregated classroom which is within the local or home school. Other children may spend part of their day "mainstreamed" into regular classes like music, P.E., art, or lunch. There are also children who are in the regular classroom (inclusion) with an aide or resource teacher available for special assistance. Others may be assigned only a portion of the daily assignment (Content Mastery).

The education of a disabled, chronically, or terminally ill child may include a variety of treatments depending on the needs of that child. There are federal and state laws which help educators provide individual programs. These laws were created so that all children's needs are met. They stipulate that each child receive a free and appropriate public education, assessment, and services. Each child should be placed in the most appropriate and least restrictive environment possible. An ARD (Admission, Review, and Dismissal) Committee meeting is held with parents. A plan is written up, called an IEP (Individual Education Plan). Generally an IEP is written with you, therapists, teachers, and any other specialists your child needs. Your school district by law should provide you with a copy of your special education rights. If there are disagreements, a legal hearing process is available to help resolve them. Your school and state also have access to advocacy agencies that may help you further. These services are usually federal or state funded and are often provided free to assist parents. Federal advocacy groups can answer your questions, or help you file claims, often free of charge. Ask your school district or refer to the numbers listed in the Appendices in the back of this book.

Some of the IEPs may include equipment, special chairs, and desks. If a child cannot hold his trunk and neck up, it will be difficult for him to learn without proper support and side arms. He may also need physical therapy to maintain and improve muscle tone and mobility. Occupational therapy may help him develop coordination to use his fine motor skills for writing or using a computer. A visual specialist may be needed to provide enlarged or special learning print for the visually impaired child. A speech therapist may help a child learn to form proper sounds and also form correct sentences that are often difficult for many children. There are also special programs if your child's illness causes hearing loss. If a child develops mental impairments, a learning specialist may assess the best ways to teach a particular child. It takes team work to provide these services. Different illness's affect how the child learns and perceives his environment. His education may be futile without team effort. This is why the IEP was developed. It can be reevaluated and altered as needed. A parent can make the request.

A child may be too weak or ill to attend a classroom setting. A home program may be implemented. The teachers or therapists can come into your home to provide this education. There are good teachers and therapists and then there are great ones. You may want to shop around. Some personality types may bring the best out in your child while others may only bring frustration. Find one who will communicate well with you and your child. You will gain the most by working cooperatively with respect for educators. However, you know your child best, and can become his greatest advocate.

HOSPITALIZATION

Often a child will need more care than a clinic visit. I have worked as a pediatric nurse in several state hospitals. I have come to appreciate the purpose, benefits, and values, along with the negative aspects of hospitalization.

In emergencies it's very comforting to have a hospital close by. When needed, your child can receive monitored medications, diagnostic information, special and nutritional diets, and therapies or treatments from a variety of professionals.

Most nurses and doctors work on the unit because they love and want to help children. This does not mean all children understand this and are happy, especially during painful treatments or procedures. Try to gather as much information as possible to prepare your child for what will happen to him/her.

Always give doctors and nurses as much information as possible about your child, including their apprehensions or fears.

A hospital must maintain some sort of routine and scheduling. This is often disruptive to you and your child. Try to understand what is expected of you and your child. Often you will be wakened for vital signs every two to four hours depending on the conditions of your child. Also meals come three times a day. Doctors and nurses make rounds and often must do a procedure or exam. Medication, treatments, and blood draws occur regularly.

Some hospitals have special units for children with the same illness. Children's cancer wards can offer children and families support during chemotherapy, surgery, bone marrow or spinal taps, and other difficult treatments. They can share pain, frustrations, hair loss, nausea, and successes with each other! Some also provide housing for the families.

MEDICAL COSTS

Unfortunately most of this help may be very expensive! We learned we had to be creative to get what Cameron needed. Our insurance company denied almost everything because, "It was over their usual and customary fee." We learned we then had to go back to different doctors and services and compare prices in our area, and resubmit claims. Through a lot of work and time (that we didn't have) we wrote letters and fought continually for services. Yet, it usually paid off.

We also humbled ourselves and wrote letters to agencies that donated money or equipment to special needs children. Easter Seals, United Cerebral Palsy, Crippled Children's Services, Shriner's services, and other local, state, and government health agencies. We qualified for some things, others we did not. (Some children may qualify for Medicaid, Title 19 Federal Waiver for special needs, ADA 612-827-2966, and Supplemental or Social Security.)

DOCTORS

There are good doctors, and then there are the really great ones. Don't be afraid to get a second opinion. Find a doctor you can talk to. A doctor that can help you understand your child's problems will benefit you, your family, and your child's educational team. A competent doctor usually has privileges at one or more hospitals. The hospitals insure he is properly licensed. If your child is under eighteen years of age, a pediatrician will be more qualified than a general practitioner. In addition, you may want a "specialist" for your child's particular problem. If your child is chronically ill or dying, you may want to make sure your doctor is easily accessible and responsive to your calls. Always strive to encourage cooperation and respect while remembering you are ultimately your child's greatest advocate.

DEALING WITH SEIZURES

Many disabled, terminally, or chronically ill children will experience seizures on a regular basis or as their death nears. Kathy McGovern kept her son at home many years. Then she sought help through partial placement. You can feel her pain and sacrifice as you hear her account of one of his frequently occurring seizures.

> The regularity of the disturbance continued to hammer at the night's silence, until the barrier between it and my sleep was finally broken. I unwillingly allowed the dull thud to enter my consciousness until I sprang from my bed with recognition. His room was right next to ours, by unexpressed design, to allow us to care for him immediately when needed. Years ago we used to take turns sitting through the nights—fearful that death would sneak in and take him without our knowledge. Now it has somehow become so routine it frightens me. At times I feel death would be a welcome assistant, but I don't allow that thought any growth. He has made our life full and unique. I seldom let the emotion of it surface, it would make the semi-normal life we've tried to carve impossible to live.
>
> His body is stiff with the upper part arched, as if to try and reach his rigged toes. His face reddens as his breath is temporarily on hold. The seconds seem like monsters, pulling at him. As the seizure starts to leave, his body twitches and jerks, hitting the side boards of the bunk bed and the wall. To avoid injury I will move him to the middle of the carpeted floor as soon as his body is at rest. A pillow will make him more comfortable, but no blanket, as the

thrashing would render it useless. I am grateful his body will be oblivious to the chill of the room.

I lift him from his bed. Trying to get eye response I call his name, "Marcus, Marcus!" Yes, there is! The recognition of my presence comforts me and gives me hope that the duration of these seizures will be short. That recognition is not always there. I shiver as I lay his head on the pillow. Remembering that my body is not oblivious to the chill, I dash to retrieve my blue house coat slung over the bed post. Why do I hurry? What is the rush? It may be a long night.

The darkness hides the light switch on the kitchen wall as my fingers search it out and flip it upward. The light offends my eyes. I pull the small green box of medications from the shelf. The promise of the drugs has never been fulfilled. Marcus' seizures have never been under complete control. I guess which ones will bring the seizures to a halt, knowing that if I'm wrong it will mean a trip to the all too familiar emergency room, or worse. Even the Emergency Room was increasing our frustration. We would count on being their three to four hours because they insist on drawing blood levels. This was easier to endure before I was made aware that we could administer the valium ourselves—at home. In place of intra-venously administering the valium, it can be given rectally in some countries. Our only choice was to allow the seizures to run their full twelve to fourteen hour course.

The thumping returned and I stepped up my pace. The sooner he swallowed these the better. The sixty seconds or so between seizures was barely enough time for me to force the pills into his mouth, raise him slightly; hopefully getting enough water in to allow the pills to slide down his throat. (Even this was a risk, I knew that, but one I was willing to take.) The water rolled down his face and was absorbed by the blue football helmet on his pajamas. Success—they're down . . . another seizure. I search for a comfortable spot but decide to pull on some socks before I continue. If I sit up I remain more alert, yet even his small bed looks comfortable.

The decision of how long to wait before making the trip to the emergency room does not have to be made with exactness. There have been times when we've gotten half way there and the seizures have subsided—there are times he's waited until arriving at the hospital and completing admission—then they have stopped. I feel so selfish, like I'm putting my needs before his when I think this way. It's an attitude unbefitting my mother-like character.

Marc's body again begins to stiffen. Is it lighter than the last? Anything strikingly different than before? Last spring, around 11 P.M., it had been different and fear had seized my heart. We called the paramedic unit and they arrived eight strong. All of us in that tiny room, watching Marc. Luckily the seizures subsided and we didn't have to transport. They were very kind and were use to being unwelcomed, yet necessary guests. They really hadn't known what to do any more than we did.

Wait, this one is exceptionally hard! How long has it lasted? He acts as though he will vomit, but something is blocking it! I hurriedly turn him on his side, praying and calling for my husband in the same breath. Suppressing fear, I recall how these seizures altered each of our lives eighteen years ago, and wonder if they will do it again now.

The joy and the many lessons he has offered our entire family could never have come to us any other way. Although he has never uttered the words "I love you" in anyone's ear, his love radiates constantly and his forgiveness is immediate. I am blessed. In reality we all walk through life on a tight rope, but certain experiences heighten our awareness of this fact. For most of us those experiences happen infrequently and at times give us a refreshing new perspective. There are some however who witness this fragileness on a near daily basis. For those, it is impossible to allow that truth to penetrate with its normal force or fear would consume our beings and render us useless. Hope of things unseen carry us from day to day and joy can enter our souls and sustain us.

When Kathy was able to let go and get help, she found new challenges. Trying to find a good residential home where there would be adequate care and protection for her son during the weekdays and some weekends was not easy. The love, concern, worry, and missing him seems to be never ending.

Another mother shared her fears about all the medications her child has to take to control his seizures. The side effects of these large doses are almost as frightening to her as his seizures. She has asked herself if he would live longer just enduring the seizures rather than all the drugs. I'm not sure there is anything more difficult than so many fears about an unknown future and watching the child you love more than anything in this world, SUFFER.

PLACEMENT

Many parents are unable to care for their disabled, chronically, or terminally ill child at home. Some will have to decide whether to place their child in an institution, group home, or hospital. This can be a difficult and a heart wrenching experience. We have watched families struggle with this decision. They receive advice from doctors, nurses, relatives, and friends. All of which can be contradictory and confusing. We have seen families place their newborn Down's syndrome infants directly into a permanent institution. We have also seen families raise a disabled or ill child for many years, then depending on the care required or their other children's needs, place that child outside their home.

We have learned not to be critical of other parents' decisions. Each child's needs and family situation is different. Parents must be helped to understand that a decision to place a child does not mean they are giving up or failing. They are admitting that they need help. Their child can still be a big part of their life. Often they can choose how much care they will give, and when they would like to take their child home, for a few hours or days.

When a child is hospitalized or institutionalized, parents may be surprised at the unique personality and qualities they discover when they visit. Many children that have challenges, develop wonderful personalities and qualities that other children may never have. And often they accept their diagnosis and future better than their parents!

Options such as where to place a child vary from state to state. I have seen some wonderful facilities with compassionate caretakers. I have also visited some institutions where I was saddened by the conditions and lack of quality care. You must decide what is best for you and your child, knowing every situation is different. You must realize friends and family may not understand or agree with what you feel is best for your child and family.

After placing a child outside your home, you may be surprised not only by the relief such help may bring, but also by the pain and grief you experience. After placing her son, Fern Kupfer said,

> Inside I ache. I keep closing the door to his room—too painful to see the crib, the diapers still in piles in the holder. Like going through a death, but not a death—thinking of him there, held and loved by strangers [1, p. 188].

In spite of this pain, she knew it was right for her and her family. She knew that if she kept him any longer she would surely break. She was reminded of this when she would bring him home on weekends.

... The clock stops ticking; everything is put on hold, as we join his world. ... the work is grueling ... six small, blended meals a day—he is fretful and scared when the swallowing doesn't come easy ... my teeth ache ... energy seeps from me ... then I cry when we all drive him back [1, p. 235].

As you can see, either placing or keeping a child at home can be a difficult decision. Each has its own set of benefits and hardships.

SURVIVING MURDER AND SUICIDE

The grief cycle may be greatly intensified when your loved one has chosen to take his/her own life, or was taken from you by murder. Research has indicated that recovery may be more complicated and longer with violent deaths such as murder or suicide. The rejection, guilt, disbelief, despair, sadness, loneliness, and anger are often frightening, overwhelming, and devastating.

You may feel uncomfortable sharing how your loved one died. You may now fear other's opinions of you or your loved one. However, you must try not to let this get in the way of your own grief work. You must allow yourself to truly mourn and let others comfort you.

"Why?" is the biggest question we want answered when anyone dies. There are rarely satisfying answers. When someone we love has chosen to take his/her own life, or has been murdered, those answers are even more confusing. It takes time to learn to live with unanswered questions. Often the mystery of the circumstances that led to their death dies with them.

The guilt or anger can be overpowering. What did we do wrong? Could we have said or done something that might have prevented this tragedy? Why would someone do this? Turning your anger or guilt into forgiveness is no easy task. However, if forgiveness isn't eventually felt, the situation/assailant has then robbed you also of future peace and recovery.

If a note was left, we wonder if they really meant what was written. If they didn't leave a note, we wish we could know what their thoughts and feelings were. Could we have helped them? What were their fears, and did they suffer? "Why, why, why?!"

Murder and suicide are both sudden and violent. The one difference between murder and suicide is that of choice. Those who lose someone to intentional destruction by another, add the problems of lack of respect for life and coping with the criminal justice system. This adds to the pain and duration one will experience. Every year 2,200 murders of one to eighteen year olds occur [2, p. 220]. One mother whose daughter was raped and murdered by a stranger said,

> It's been seven years . . . you never forget it, you just learn to live with the pain. It's something you don't just get over.

This kind of chronic of "shadow grief" is common to parents who have lost children [3, p. 40], I think one could assume especially in sudden, violent deaths. You may receive help by contacting Parents of Murdered Children, Inc., 1739 Bella Vista, Cincinnati, Ohio 45237—531-242-8025.

I've seen reports indicating that as many as 500,000 teenagers attempt suicide annually. Researchers suggest that 5,000-6,000 succeed in taking their lives [2, p. 186]. Adults attempt suicide at about the same frequency, however, are about five times more likely to succeed. Suicide also is the fifth cause of death among five to fourteen year olds! [2, p. 186].

Suicide is usually a response to some perceived pain that your loved one felt could not be solved in any other way. Yet simple answers may not comfort us. Marilyn Dickson explains,

> Once a person intentionally chooses suicide as the path to take, there is nothing you (or anyone) could have done to change his/her mind. From their perspective, the pain of daily living overwhelms the promise that life holds and no hope is offered for anything better [4].

Because their decision brings them a sense of relief, they may follow through quickly without efforts to explain or say good-bye. The intensity of their pain is hard for others to grasp or comprehend. Even when we realize they may not have understood totally what they were doing, and are probably not accountable for their actions, our hearts are broken. We are now the ones left to cope and pick up the pieces.

> Karen Athay Packer compared the suicide of her loved one with a beautiful ceramic bowl he had made and given to her before his death. It had broken soon after. Her daughter saw the pieces in the garbage. Crying, she said, "It is just like what happened to him. I looked down and saw his life lying there in the bottom of the garbage, like something thrown out because no one knew what to do with it. Tomorrow they'll come and take it away, and I can't bear for that to happen. I want you to save the pieces. Even if they're

broken, they are still beautiful." Her mother, stunned by her sensitive daughter's feelings learned a great lesson. She had judged her loved one's whole life as negative because he chose suicide. She had discounted all the good memories, all the wonderful times and things he had done for her and others. She hurried and got out the flash light and went out to the garbage. "Yes, I will save all the pieces, even though I can't put them together, even though I can't make all the fragments fit." Even though she couldn't understand her father's choice, the pieces of his life still had beauty and important memories for her. She was able to face the negative feelings, yet still hold on to the positive memories. She now felt God could put the beautiful pieces of her father's soul together and she could love him and go on with more peace [5, pp. 52-54].

When my mother-in-law's children found her lifeless body in the garage after she committed suicide, they immediately started CPR (cardiopulmonary resuscitation). It was too late for her to be resuscitated and the visual memory of seeing their mother in that condition will always haunt them. I like Jeannette Partridge's quote from her booklet, "Losing a Loved One," where she makes this analogy about how slow and dark the recovery can be.

Then, finally you begin to see light at the end of the long black tunnel—and you grope your way toward that light. Sometimes in your journey, the light dims and you're not even sure it is there. At other times, the light becomes brighter and you want to hurry toward it, for with it comes the sense of purpose and well-being that you have perhaps not felt for a long time. The length of the tunnel varies with different situations and different people, but all of those I have spoken with do find themselves in this tunnel and do see the light eventually [6, p. 10].

The following is a letter written to a young girl by Peggy Benedict, who herself had experienced the death of two loved ones by suicide. It displays the many fears and feelings suicide brings to those left behind.

Dear Mary,

Your mom told me today of your recent loss. I can't tell you how much I am thinking of you. I may not be able to help you because loss and grief are often a personal, and private thing. I just want you to know it may take a long time for you to understand why your friend would take her own life.

Twice in my life I have been exposed to death by suicide. Once when I was sixteen, and my boyfriend shot himself. Again at age thirty-five my own father hung himself. It is very hard to understand how someone could possibly hurt so much to even contemplate something so final, much less follow through. The one that is gone may feel less pain than those left behind. There are so many emotions that those left behind feel, I hope I can put to words some of mine.

First there is anger, "How dare you! You didn't really have it so bad, why couldn't you deal with it all?" Were they just not strong enough to deal with what ever life handed them? They must have felt so bad they really saw no other way out. Maybe someday we'll understand some of their pain, but now the solution they chose seems so foreign.

Secondly, you may feel as though if you would have been there, done, or said something different you might have prevented it all. Unfortunately those who commit suicide hurt so badly and so deeply that they sometimes refuse to seek or even allow a good friend to help them through. It may take you a while if you feel this guilt to heal, yet with time and patience you can.

There may also be feelings of embarrassment. Suicide is generally viewed as unacceptable thing to do. It is difficult to explain to others. Someone told me when my boyfriend died, "That at least it was his and his alone choice to die." I believe this helped me because it was so difficult to think about this very young vivacious person taken away from me and others who loved him. It has been many years for me but I still avoid mentioning how my dad died. I am not sure if I will ever get over these feelings, but as the years go by it is easier.

The next few months will be very difficult for you, your families, and all who cared for her. Your mother and father are very caring. I hope you will choose to talk to them frequently about your feelings. Talking about it, crying, expressing your emotions will help you sort out these feelings and head toward a level of understanding. Remember the good times and all the positive things you saw. If I can help you, or be a listening ear, I am here for you. Know that my thoughts are with you during this very difficult time in your life.

For awhile, you may just go through the motions of everyday living. Functioning at even the simplest level may be frightening. If your child chose suicide over chronic or terminal illness you may suffer mixed feelings of guilt and ambivalence along with your confusion.

Many caretakers, including parents, have anticipated the death of their terminally ill child. They fear or wonder if one day they won't wake up from their nap, or won't recover from a serious fall. Some exhausted parents have thought of suicide as an escape from the difficult situations they are in. Fern Kupfer in her book, *Before and After Zachariah,* tells about one mother who said,

> I know that when I get too down, and I really can't take it anymore, that I always have suicide as an option, that at least I have a choice about that. Then she adds that she would probably have to take her chronically ill child with her! [1, p. 84].

These parents need a lot of help and understanding. Many don't know where to turn for the help they need, or are afraid to ask for help. They may wish to contact the American Association of Suicidology, Suite 310, 4201 Connecticut Ave., N.W., Washington, D.C., 20008 for support and information.

There are several accounts of near-death experiences from individuals who had committed suicide, died and returned (see Chapter 8). Some of these people claimed the problems they were trying to leave behind seemed to still be there for them to work on. They didn't feel condemned for their life or choices. They felt an unconditional love, understanding, forgiveness, and acceptance. They came to know life was important and felt more determined that they had things to accomplish. Their recovery seemed to bring them more meaning and purpose for staying alive, and no fear of death. They felt greater faith and hope for their future here and after death.

Could this faith and hope lead to the feelings expressed by a woman who wrote in her journal before her death a description of a ship sailing out to sea:

> As it nears the horizon some say, "There, It's gone!" Gone where? Gone from sight—that is all. The ship is just as large in mast and hull and spar as it ever was when it left my side, and just as able to bear the load of its living freight to the destination for which it was sent.
>
> Its diminished size is in me, not in the ship itself; and just at the moment when someone at my side says, "There, she is gone!" There are other eyes watching her coming, and other voices ready to take up the glad shout, "There, the ship comes!" and that is DYING! [4].

REFERENCES

1. F. Kupfer, *Before and After Zachariah,* Delacorte Press, New York, 1971.
2. G. Anderson, *Our Children Forever,* Berkley Books, New York, 1994.
3. R. L. Knapp, *Beyond Endurance: When a Child Dies,* Schocken Books, New York, 1986.
4. M. Dickson, *Grief Recovery Seminars,* Dallas, Texas, 1991.
5. The Ensign Magazine, Salt Lake City, Utah, September 1992.
6. J. Partridge *Losing a Loved One,* Olympus Publishing Co., Salt Lake City, Utah, 1989.

APPENDIX

Resources and Organizations

DISABILITIES/EDUCATION

Division for Physical and Health Disabilities/
  Clearinghouse for Professions in Special Education
1920 Association Drive
Reston, VA 22091-1589
703-620-3660

Association for Children and Adults with Learning Disabilities
4156 Library Road
Pittsburgh, PA 15234
412-341-1515

Clearinghouse on Disability Information/
  Office of Special Education & Rehabilitative Services
Switzer Blvd. Room 3132
Washington, D.C. 20202-2524
202-205-8241

Christian League for the Handicapped
P.O. Box 948
Walworth, WI 53184-0943
414-275-6131

Accent on Information
P.O. Box 700
Bloomington, IL 61702
309-378-2961

National Information Center for Children
  & Youth with Disabilities
P.O. Box 1492
Washington, D.C. 20013
800-695-0285

Health Resource Center
1 Dupont Cir. Ste. 800
Washington, D.C. 20036-1193
800-544-3284

Association on Higher Education and Disability
P.O. Box 21192
Columbus, OH 43221-0192
614-488-4972

American Disability Association
2121 8th Ave. Ste. 1623
Birmingham, AL 35203
205-323-3030

March of Dimes
1275 Mamaroneck Avenue
White Plains, NY 10605
914-428-7100

Easter Seal Society
230 W. Monroe St. #1800
Chicago, IL 60601
312-726-6200

National Organization on Disability
910 16th St. #600
Washington, D.C. 20006
202-293-5960

SPECIFIC DISABILITIES

The Encyclopedia of Associations 1996 edition at your local library lists specific problems. Here are a few examples:

The United Cerebral Palsy Assoc., Inc.
1660 L St. N.W. #700
Washington, D.C. 20036-5602
202-842-1266

Mental Retardation Association of America, Inc.
211 East 300 S. #212
Salt Lake City, UT 84111
801-328-1575

Association of Birth Defect Child, Inc.
827 Irma Ave.
Orlando, FL 32803
407-245-7035
800-313-2232

National Down Syndrome Society
666 Broadway
New York, NY 10012
800-221-4602

Cystic Fibrosis Foundation
6931 Arlington, Rd. #200
Bethesda, MD 20814
800-344-4823

Parents of Amputee Children Together
1199 Pleasant Valley Way
West Orange, NJ 07052
201-731-8400

National Library Service for the Blind and Physically Handicapped
1291 Taylor St. NW
Washington, D.C. 20542
202-707-5100

Parent Helping Parents: The Family Resource Center
3041 Olcott St.
Santa Clara, CA 90504-3222
408-727-5775

CHRONIC/TERMINAL ILLNESS

The Encyclopedia of Associations 1996 edition at your local library lists specific illnesses.

National Health Information Clearinghouse
P.O. Box 1133
Washington, D.C. 20013-1133
800-336-4797

Make a Wish Foundation of America
100 West Claredon #2200
Phoenix, AZ 85013
800-332-9474

Direct Link
P.O. Box 1036
Solvang, CA
805-688-1603

National Hospice Organization
1901 North Moore St. #901
Arlington, VA 22209
703-234-5900

American Brain Tumor Association
2720 River Road
Des Plaines, IL 60018
800-886-2282
708-827-9910

National AIDS/American Social Health Associations
P.O. Box 13827
Research Triangle Park, NC 27709
800-342-AIDS

National Maternal and Child Health Clearinghouse
8201 Greensboro Dr. Ste. 600
McLean, VA 22102-3810
703-821-8955

National Organization for
  Rare Disorders
P.O. Box 8923
New Fairfield, CT 06812-8923
800-999-NORD

AHCPR (Health)
P.O. Box 8547
Silver Springs, MD 20907-8547
800-358-9295

American Cancer Society
777 Third Ave.
New York, NY 10017
212-586-8700
or
1-800-227-2345

Cancer Information Clearinghouse
9000 Rockville Pike
Bld. 31 Room 10A21
Bethesda, MD 20205
800-4-CANCER

Children With Special Health
  Care Needs Program
Parklawn Bld.
5600 Fishers Ln. Room 18A27
Rockville, MD 20857
301-443-2350

National AIDS Hotline
P.O. Box 13827
Research Triangle Park, NC 27709
800-342-AIDS

INFANT LOSS

RTS Bereavement Services
1910 South Avenue
La Crosse, WI 54601
800-362-9567

SIDS Alliance
1314 Bedford Ave. #210
Baltimore, MD 21208
800-221-SIDS

Pregnancy and Infant Loss Center
1421 E. Wayzara Blvd. #30
Wayzata, MN 55391
612-473-9372

AMEND
4324 Berrywick Terrace
St. Louis, MO 63128
314-487-7582

Share
300 1st Capitol Drive
St. Charles, MO 63301
314-947-6164

LOSS OF A CHILD

The National Organization
  of Compassionate Friends
P.O. Box 3696
Oak Brook, IL 60522-3696
708-990-0010

MADD
511 E. John Carpenter
  Freeway #700
Irving, TX 75062
800-438-MADD

The Candlelighters Childhood
  Cancer
7910 Woodmont Ave. #460
Bethesda, MD 20814
301-657-8401

Parents Reaching Out
P.O. Box 121806
Nashville, TN 37212-1806

Rainbows
1111 Tower Rd.
Schaumburg, ID 60173-4305
708-310-1880

Parents of Murdered Children
100 E. 8th St. B-41
Cincinnati, OH 45202
513-721-5683

HOPE
1215 E. Michigan Ave.
P.O. Box 30480
Lansing, MI 48909

Parents Helping Parents
3041 Olcott St.
Santa Clara, CA 905054-3222

LOSS OF SPOUSE

Widowed Persons Service
(under AARP Dept.)
601 E. Street N.W.
Washington, D.C. 20049
202-434-2277

LOSS OF SIBLING

The National Organization of
Compassionate Friends
P.O. Box 3696
Oak Brook, IL 60522-3696
708-990-0010

LOSS OF PARENTS

National Hospice Organization
1901 North Moore St. #901
Arlington, VA 22209
703-234-5900

SUICIDE

American Association of
Suicidology
Suite 310
4201 Connecticut Ave., N.W.
Washington, D.C. 20008
202-237-2280

American Suicide Foundation
1045 Park Ave.
New York, NY 10028-1030
800-531-4477

Seasons: Suicide Bereavement
P.O. Box 187
Park City, Utah 84060
801-649-8331

FEDERAL ADVOCACY GROUPS

Legal Center Serving Disabilities
455 Sherman St. #130
Denver, CO 08203
303-722-0300

Governmental Affairs Office
1522 K St., N.W. #516
Washington, D.C. 20005

ACCD
1200 15th St. N.W. #201
Washington, D.C. 20005

Parent Information Center
P.O. Box 1422
Concord, NH 03302-1422
603-224-7005

DISABILITIES TOY CATALOGS

Kapable Kids Inc.
P.O. Box 250
Bohemia, NY 11716
800-356-1564
515-563-7176

Rifton Equipment
P.O. Box 901, Rt. 213
Rifton, NY 10014
800-374-3866
914-658-8065

Community Playthings
P.O. Box 901
Rifton, NY 12471
914-658-8065
800-777-4244

Abilitations
One Sportime Way
Atlanta, GA 30340-1402
1-800-850-8602

Early Intervention
Order Service Center
P.O. Box 839954
San Antonio, TX 78283-3954
800-228-0752 or 602-323-7500

Also educational school supply stores often have special toys and equipment.

HOME CARE CATALOGS

Adapt Ability
P.O. Box 515
Colchester, CT 06415
1-800-243-9232

Enrichments
145 Tower Drive
P.O. Box 579
Hinsdale, IL 60521
708-393-4030

Fred Sammons Inc.
145 Tower Dr., Dept. 381
Burr Ridge, IL 60521-9842
708-328-1700

Rifton Equipment
P.O. Box 901, Rt. 213
Rifton, NY 10014
800-374-3866
914-658-8065

About the Authors

Joyce Marsden Ashton is a Registered Pediatric Nurse and Certified Grief Counselor. She leads the Caring and Sharing Support Group for parents experiencing miscarriage, stillborn, ectopic pregnancy, or newborn death.

Dennis Dale Ashton has his Master's Degree in Clinical Social Work and is a Board Certified Licensed Psychotherapist. He is the Director of a Social Service Agency with offices in Dallas and Houston, Texas.

The Ashton's are both professionals who speak and give workshops on Marriage Relationships, Self-Esteem, Caring for the Disabled and Terminally Ill, Effective Parenting, Abuse, Adoption and Infertility, Dealing with Depression and Anxiety, Loss and Grief Recovery. They are the parents of six children, four are living. Their hobbies include camping, boating, biking, swimming, aerobics, snow and water skiing.

INDEX

Absence of grief, 124
Abuse, 4, 9, 10, 85, 110, 140
Accept/acceptance, 8, 17-22, 27, 37,
    40, 42-44, 50-51, 53-
    54, 62, 70, 75, 81, 84, 91-92,
    96, 99, 102, 106, 109-110,
    114, 117, 119, 126-127, 131,
    133, 134, 137, 145, 167, 172
Acting out (children), 123
Actualizing a loss, 93 (see also Loss)
Addiction, 10, 50, 124
Adoption, 6, 7, 9, 84, 93
Adversity (see Challenges)
Advocacy, 29-30, 161-162 (see also
    Legal/advocacy)
Affection (see Touch)
Aging, 10
Agree to disagree, 111
"All or nothing" thinking, 116
Angels, 75, 138, 140, 151, 154
Angry/anger, 15, 18, 27, 38, 45,
    57-58, 72, 74-76, 80, 84, 86,
    89, 92, 97, 99, 100, 102, 104,
    112, 117-119, 122, 124, 132,
    134, 135, 149, 168
  bitter/bitterness, 45, 72, 86, 100,
    124
Anxious/anxiety, 9, 11, 14, 25, 50,
    51, 72-73, 75, 79, 80, 83-84,
    86, 89, 99, 102-103
  separation anxiety, 25, 119

Apgar score, 13
Appearance/body image, 52, 53, 58,
    61, 62, 123
ARD (Admission, Review,
    Dismissal), 161
Aspirated, 13, 78
Asthma, 5, 148
Atonement, 96, 133, 159
Attitude, 10, 39, 45, 49, 52, 98, 142,
    165 [see also Positive
    thoughts or attitude;
    Negative (feelings)]

Balance, finding a, 38, 39, 54, 84,
    94, 125, 142
Bargaining, 84, 85, 111
Bathing/dressing, 28, 30, 35-36,
    51, 53, 62, 64, 66, 78-79, 93,
    131
Bereaved, 97-99, 102-103, 115, 121
    (see also Mourning; Grief;
    Pain and hurt)
  graph, 104-105
Blind, 16, 151-152
Body massage, 113
Boy Scouts, 60
Brain, 70, 78-79, 80, 92, 115-116,
    122, 140, 144 (see also
    Cognitive and Thoughts)

Cancer, 40, 147, 163, 178, 179

Cardiopulmonary resuscitation (CPR), 3, 4, 13, 66, 136-137, 155, 170

Caretaker, 91, 124, 167

Cerebral palsy, 8, 14, 62, 65, 121, 149, 150

Challenges (adversity, trials, tragedies, trauma and limitations), 3, 4, 7, 8, 10, 14, 15, 22, 28, 37, 40, 41, 45, 46, 50-52, 53, 56, 58, 61, 64, 66, 70, 73, 81, 85, 88, 94, 97, 98, 99, 109, 113, 115, 116, 118, 127-128, 132-135, 139-140, 142, 150, 152, 157, 158, 166

Change, 6, 7, 8, 10, 13, 15, 22, 35, 39, 45, 56-57, 61, 63, 74, 81, 87, 91, 94-95, 97-98, 102-103, 106, 109, 112, 117, 119-120, 126, 129, 169

Choices, 75, 81, 129, 133, 139, 170, 172 (see also Decisions)

Church/clergy, 43, 50, 72, 75, 85, 86, 94, 101, 132-134, 143, 156, 157

Cliches (platitudes), 74, 99, 100, 118, 149

Cognitive/mind, 62, 70, 73, 78-79, 80, 92, 115-116, 122, 140, 144 (see also Thoughts and Brain)

Communication (express/talk), 13, 20, 22, 28, 33, 37, 40-46, 51, 55-58, 61-62, 64, 78-79, 82-83, 87-88, 92-93, 99-100, 102-103, 110-115, 118-124, 124, 127, 137, 141, 144, 146-147, 150, 155-156, 162, 164, 171

Compartmental thinking, 116

Compulsive behavior and thinking, 39, 50

Conflict, 20, 26, 111, 114

Confusion and lack of concentration, 4, 9, 14, 15, 61, 71-75, 79, 84, 86, 91, 93, 99, 105, 113, 115, 116, 120, 122-123, 132-134, 140, 145, 149, 150, 153, 167-168, 171 (see also Disorientation/ disorganization)

Constructive criticism, 111

Control, 21, 27, 49, 53, 70, 75, 78, 79-84, 92, 100, 112, 140

letting go, 81-83, 92, 111, 112, 123, 125, 127

loss of, 3-6, 9, 10, 18, 21, 70, 78-81, 84, 124, 131, 135, 154

of thoughts, 50, 79, 93, 99 (see also Thoughts)

over control, 55, 80-81, 120

Cooperation, 112

Coping and surviving, 22-23, 98, 149

Corner seat illustration, 30, 31

Criminal justice system, 168

Criticism, 112

constructive criticism, 111

Crying/tears, 3, 10, 13, 14, 19, 29, 34, 37, 51, 58, 63, 73-75, 77, 79, 83, 91, 93, 95, 97, 100-102, 104, 113-115, 119, 122, 125-127, 143-144, 146-148, 153, 154, 156, 168-169, 171

Cystic fibrosis, 19, 52, 148-149

Death, die, dying, 3, 4, 7, 8, 11, 12, 15, 17-19, 26, 27, 29, 40-42, 45-46, 52, 60, 63-64, 66, 69, 72-78, 80-81, 83-85, 87-89, 91-92, 97-100, 102-105, 107, 112-113, 115-118, 119, 120-125, 128, 131-133, 135, 136-138, 140-150, 152, 153-155, 159, 164, 167-169, 171-172

[Death, die, dying]
"a time to die," 139
accidental death, 16, 139, 142
Death preparations, 149, 150
Decisions, 6, 29, 41, 70, 77, 80, 84,
    87-88, 92, 99, 101-102, 118,
    148, 153, 165, 167-169 (see
    also Choices)
Denial/disbelief, 3, 8, 13, 14, 18-19,
    29, 43, 45, 70-74, 84, 89, 97,
    101, 119, 126
Depression/despair, 6, 9, 18, 19, 40,
    45, 50, 60, 71-73, 75, 79-80,
    84, 86, 89, 92, 97, 98, 100,
    103, 105, 119, 121, 122,
    124-125, 156, 168
Detachment, 27, 123
Developmental
    growth/developmentally, 8,
    13, 14, 16, 28, 29, 31-33, 54
Developmental delays, 14, 119, 139
    physical delays, 38
Diagnosis, 6, 7, 8, 9, 11-13, 15, 16,
    21, 126, 131, 148
    acceptance of, 22-30, 158, 167
    delayed, 12-15, 16, 25
    denial of, 18, 19
    of grief, 69
    of spiritual problems, 156
    social isolation from, 19-20
    struggle with, 11-23
    telling the child of, 21-22
    unknown diagnosis, 6, 11, 12 (see
        also Testing)
Differences
    between faith and grief, 133-134
    between men and women, 7, 109,
        113-117
    between spirituality and religion,
        134-135
Disabilities/disabled, 4, 9, 10, 11,
    16, 17, 19-22, 25-27, 29,
    33-46, 49, 53, 56-57, 62, 78,
    80, 88-89, 92-93, 109, 112,
    116, 132, 139, 142, 151-152,
    161, 163-164, 167

Discipline, 38, 54-55, 123
Disorientation/disorganization, 71,
    85-86, 105 (see Confusion)
Distorted grief, 124
Divorce, 4, 7, 8, 10, 109, 110
Doctors, 6, 8, 9, 12, 13, 15-16,
    18-22, 26-27, 29, 33, 42, 51,
    65, 75, 77-78, 102-103, 121,
    126, 131, 136-137, 144, 148,
    155-156, 163-164, 167
Downs syndrome, 116, 167
Dreams/hopes, 10, 11, 15, 63, 83
    night dreams, 60, 141, 143-146,
        154, 159
Duration (length) of grief, 9, 73, 74,
    84, 89, 103-105, 109, 114,
    116, 126, 132, 134, 168
Duration of seizures, 165

Eating/feeding problems, 13-15,
    28-32, 37, 39, 43, 59, 65,
    72, 80, 82, 94, 119, 123,
    131, 137, 143, 156, 161,
    163, 168
    appetite changes in stress and
        grief, 79
Education/school/teachers/special
    education, 20-22, 26-27,
    29-40, 50-52, 54, 59, 62-65,
    69, 77, 83, 85, 88, 115,
    119-121, 124, 126-127,
    128, 131, 134, 141, 143, 145,
    147, 152, 156, 158, 161-162,
    164
Emotional investment, 9, 73, 86, 97
Emotions, 9, 17, 20, 29, 51, 56,
    70-73, 75, 78, 82, 87, 93,
    96-98, 103-105, 109, 114,
    117-120, 123, 132-133, 143,
    164 (see also Feelings)
    children "acting out," 123
    graph (emotional dimensions and
        symptoms), 71
Endorphins/serotonin, 80, 92

Equipment, 8, 14, 19, 21, 30-33, 35-37, 39, 40, 44, 46, 52, 59, 62-65, 74, 77, 131, 141-142

Exercise, 32, 35, 77, 80, 82, 85, 94, 120, 156

Faith/hope, 8, 14, 15, 17, 19, 26-27, 34-35, 45-46, 60, 64, 72, 78-79, 86, 88, 94-96, 98, 131-135, 138, 140, 145, 148, 149, 152, 154-159, 166, 169, 172
  difference in faith and grief, 133-134

False self, 86, 100 (see also Masks)

Family, friends, relatives, 4, 6, 8, 10, 16, 19, 20, 26, 28, 34-35, 37-39, 41-44, 55, 57, 61, 63, 64, 72-75, 80-81, 85-88, 89, 92, 95, 97-98, 100, 101-103, 109-112, 114, 116, 120, 122, 124-127, 129, 134, 137, 139, 140, 142-144, 147, 149, 151-152, 154-155, 163-164, 166, 167, 170, 171
  dead relatives appear, 137

Fear, 6, 11, 13, 16, 18-22, 26, 41-43, 46, 60, 73, 75, 80, 99, 100, 102, 117, 119, 120, 122-124, 132, 137, 142, 144, 149, 155, 163-164, 166, 168, 170-172 (see also Panic attacks; Post-traumatic stress syndrome)

Feelings, 8, 14-16, 20, 22, 27, 41-43, 45-46, 50-52, 55-58, 61, 64, 69-71, 73, 75, 78, 79, 85-86, 91-93, 97, 104, 110-112, 116-117, 119, 120, 122-124, 129, 135-137, 139, 141, 148, 149, 150-151, 153-154 (see also Emotions)
  ambiguous feelings, 27, 104, 171 (see also Negative feelings)
  graph, 71

Forgiveness/Forgiving, 75, 79, 94, 112, 133-135, 138, 166, 168, 172

Foster care, 27-29

Funeral, 43, 87-89, 92, 117-120, 132, 146, 149-150

Future, 10, 11, 21, 23, 35, 45, 83, 92, 98, 119-120, 127, 139, 143-144, 150, 166, 172

Goals (achievements, abilities, achieve accomplishments, performance), 21, 49-53, 55-57, 60-61, 63-65, 85, 99, 126, 139

God, 45, 51, 55, 59, 63-64, 70, 72, 74-76, 81, 86, 99, 118, 131-134, 140-142, 146, 148-149, 152, 157, 159
  "Light," 137, 138

Gratitude therapy, 93, 130, 151

Grief, 12, 15, 54, 66, 69, 72, 73-74, 78, 80, 83, 85-87, 92-95, 96, 99, 101, 107, 109, 112, 113, 116-117, 120-121, 123-126, 130, 132-134, 139, 143, 145, 147-148, 156, 157-158, 167-168
  absence of grief, 124
  anticipatory grief, 18, 27, 45, 172
  complicated grief, 9, 69, 75, 86, 97-98, 118, 123, 132, 168
    in siblings, 124
  differences in grief and faith, 133-134
  grief attacks, 93-95
  grief work, 70, 82, 85, 88, 91-92, 97, 99, 103, 118, 127
  recovery/healing, 73, 84-87, 89, 112, 113, 117, 134 (see also Chapters 6 and 8)
  recovery of children, 117-124
  shadow grief, 94, 96, 169
  symptoms, stages, process, 70, 90, 104-105, 118
    graph, 71

Guilt/shame, 16, 18, 26-27, 29, 41,
    65, 72, 75-79, 87, 89, 97, 99,
    102-105, 119, 121-124,
    132-134, 142, 144, 168, 171
  false guilt, 78-79, 80

Hallucinations, 136
Happiness (*see* Joy, peace, and
    happiness)
Healing (*see* Grief recovery)
Hearing (*see* Speech/vision/
    hearing)
Heaven, 75, 95, 141, 146, 150,
    154
Helping others (*see* Serving Others)
Holidays and special occasions, 4,
    93-96, 100, 143
Home care, 22, 25, 27, 30, 32,
    34-36, 39, 162
Honesty, 17, 21, 40-41, 43, 46, 55,
    57, 61, 110, 111, 118-120,
    127, 143-145
Hormones, 116-117
Hospice, 27
Hospitals, 12, 21, 26-27, 62, 65-66,
    85, 97, 102, 121, 132, 137,
    144, 148, 150, 155-156, 162,
    163, 165, 167
Humor, 45, 60, 62, 64, 124, 125,
    134

Identity, 21, 56, 62
  lost identity, 82, 86, 114
  new identity, 130 (*see also* New
      normal/new identity)
IEP (Individual Educational Plan),
    161-162
Illness, 4, 6-11, 14-22, 26-27, 29-36,
    40, 42-45, 49, 53, 55-57, 61,
    75, 79, 84-85, 87, 109,
    112-114, 125, 127, 137,
    141-142, 155-156, 161-162,
    163-164, 167

Impressions/intuitions/
    premonitions, 56-57, 141,
    145, 148-155 (*see also*
    Revelations)
Infertility, 4, 6, 7, 9, 10
Inner child, 82, 86, 129
Institutional care, 161, 167
Insurance/claims, 42, 163
Intellectual/mental, 9, 42, 70, 73,
    78, 81-82, 97, 103, 109, 113,
    121, 133, 156
  graph (dimensions and symptoms
      of), 71
IQ scores, 25
Irony, 77, 131
Isolation, 19, 20, 86-87, 99, 102,
    119, 127, 133 (*see also*
    Withdrawal)

Jaw control, 14, 30
Jesus Christ, 88, 95-96, 99, 144,
    148, 150-152, 159
Journals (*see* Reading/writing)
Joy, peace, and happiness, 4, 6, 7,
    23, 29, 37, 40-41, 44-46,
    49-53, 55, 58-59, 64-65,
    72-73, 80, 84-86, 88-91, 93,
    99-103, 112, 114, 116-119,
    124-126, 129, 131-132,
    135-140, 142-147, 149,
    151-154, 159, 168, 170 (*see
    also* Love)
Judge/judgment, 112, 137

Knowledge, 12, 16-17, 22, 34, 70,
    117, 134-136, 154-155,
    157-158, 164

Laws, natural, 133, 149
Legal/advocacy, 29-30, 161-162, 181
Leukemia, 150, 178, 179 (*see also*
    Cancer)

Life review (Cameron's), 59-66
   in NDEs, 138
Life support, 144
Listen/listening, 42, 57, 88, 98,
     102-103, 110, 115, 120, 122,
     126, 127, 134, 171
   reflective listening, 110-112
Loneliness, 8, 42, 73, 86, 94, 99, 168
Longing, yearning, pining, 83, 84,
     104 (*see also* Searching/
     asking why?)
Loss, 7, 21, 73, 79-80, 90, 93-98,
     103, 109, 117, 120-121,
     132, 134-135, 170 (*see also*
     Death)
   multiple loss, 8, 10, 17, 70
   of appetite, 79
   of child, 3-6, 9-10, 15, 45, 46, 69,
     77, 84, 86, 91, 139, 147, 148,
     180
   of control, 3-4, 6, 10, 18, 21, 53,
     69, 78-81, 84, 124, 131, 135
   of energy, 79
   of finances, 4, 10, 53
   of friends, 110
   of home/moving, 4, 5, 8-10, 120
   of identity, 8, 10, 86
   of infant, 5, 6, 10, 12, 74, 75, 84,
     92, 106, 149, 180
   of job, 4, 5, 8, 10, 115, 120
   of parents, 4-6, 10, 180
   of pets, 5, 10
   of sexual desire, 79, 112-113
   of spouse, 5, 6, 10, 181, 182
Loss scales, 4, 5, 69
   kinds of loss scale, 10
   stages, duration, and intensity of
     loss scale, 104-105
Love, 16, 39, 44, 61, 63, 65, 73, 75,
     86-89, 100-103, 110-113,
     115, 117, 119, 120, 123, 126,
     129, 131, 133-134, 136, 138,
     144, 152, 155, 158-159, 170
     (*see also* Joy, peace, and
     happiness)

[Love]
   unconditional love, 6, 51, 53-55,
     58, 134, 138, 172

Magical thinking, 22
Mainstreaming/inclusion, 34,
     36-38, 161
Marriage, 20, 82, 107, 109, 117
   marital discord, 20, 114-117, 157
   spouse, 6, 41, 81, 109-115, 129,
     181
   spouse observation checklist, 111
Masks, 86, 100-102 (*see also* False
     self)
Meaning/purpose, 9, 44-46, 52, 58,
     64, 75, 81, 85, 93, 95, 97,
     111, 119-120, 128-129,
     135-136, 152-153, 158-159,
     170, 172
   new meaning, 97 (*see also* New
     normal/new identity)
Medical costs, 42, 163
Medications, 18, 26-28, 38, 42,
     45-46, 66, 74, 77, 92, 103,
     162, 163, 165-166
Meditation, 82, 113, 129, 144, 156
   (*see also* Prayer)
Memories, 74, 83, 85, 94, 99-100,
     102, 120, 143, 170
Men (*see also* Differences)
   characteristics of, 114-116
   loss of power and protector role,
     114
Mental retardation or delays, 14,
     16, 25, 128, 139, 162
   IQ scores, 25
"Mind, body, soul," 155-156
Miracles, 19, 34, 51, 112, 133, 151,
     155
Miscarriage, 4, 6, 7, 10, 12, 84
Mourn/mourning, 42, 80, 91, 95-97,
     99, 104-105, 123, 132-133,
     148, 153, 159, 168 (*see also*
     Bereaved/grief)

Multiple loss (accumulative effect), 8, 10, 17, 70
Murder, 10, 77, 168-169, 180
Music, 39, 82, 87, 113, 120, 161

Nausea, 32, 163, 166
NDEs (near death experiences), 46, 135-136, 139, 140,147, 155, 172
  in children, 140
Negative
  feelings, 42-43, 45, 75, 111, 117, 122, 124, 127, 129-130, 133-135, 170
  labels, 16, 56-58, 61, 129
  thoughts, 45, 58, 80-81, 112, 117
  words, 58, 112
New normal/new identity, 71, 84, 86, 92-93, 97, 106, 130
Next life, 46, 64, 72, 135, 141-142, 145, 149-150, 152, 155, 158-159
Nurse, 3, 6, 8, 11-13, 15-16, 21, 23, 29, 34, 66, 78, 93, 131, 136, 155, 162-163, 167

Oral stimulation, 30 (see also Eating/Feeding)
Organizations and resources, 25, 42, 163, 175-182
Over activity, 80, 85

Pain/hurt, 4, 6, 9, 10, 12, 16, 17, 29, 40, 42, 45, 58, 65-66, 69, 73-75, 77-78, 84, 86-87, 91, 94-97, 99-101, 110, 112-113, 116-117, 120, 123, 125, 127, 131, 133-137, 143, 147, 149, 151, 156-157, 159, 163, 167-169, 171
Panic attacks, 73, 119, 124

Parents, 4, 6, 7, 8, 12, 15-17, 19, 22, 25-28, 34, 40, 42-45, 49-52, 54-57, 61, 70, 72-73, 75, 77, 84-85, 89, 94, 98, 106, 109, 118, 120-124, 135, 139-140, 142, 144-145, 147, 150, 152, 161-162, 167, 169, 171
  loss of, 181
Photo therapy, 80
Physical
  illness, 73, 103, 123
  pain, 129
  retardation, 139, 152
  symptoms of grief, 70-73, 97, 133
  in children, 119
  graph, 71
Placement, 25, 164, 167
Platitudes (see Cliches)
Play, 31, 43-44, 59, 63-65, 83, 91, 118-119
PMS (Pre-menstrual syndrome), 116-117
Positive thoughts or attitude, 22, 38, 40, 41, 45, 54, 57, 62, 64, 80, 81, 93, 117, 122, 128-130, 142, 144, 147, 171
Post-traumatic stress syndrome, 73, 116
Power
  of faith, 158-159
  struggles, 112, 120, 124
Powerlessness, 126
Prayer, 64, 80, 87, 97, 131, 135, 138, 142, 147-148, 150, 153, 158-159, 166 (see also Meditation)
Pregnancy, 41
  unwed, 4, 10
Pride/proud, 52, 112, 142
Principles, 55, 61, 64, 94, 119, 157-158
Professionals, 8, 9, 12, 14-16, 17-19, 25, 77-78, 80, 86, 91, 101, 115, 120, 123-124, 129, 136, 147-148, 153, 156-158, 162

Psychology, 115, 156-158
Psychotherapy, 92, 101, 115, 147, 153, 156-158

Reading/writing/journals, 16-17, 28, 44-45, 61, 63, 65, 74, 75, 79-80, 89, 94, 112, 120, 135, 141, 146, 150, 154-156, 159, 162, 168, 172
Rebellious children, 4, 10
Recovery/healing (*see also* Grief recovery)
Recreation/relaxation, 39-40, 80, 113, 137
Regression, 123-124
Relationships, 3, 6, 7, 9, 10, 20, 35, 54-56, 70, 97, 98, 109-130, 134
Remissions/relapses, 26, 38, 75, 123
Repression/"stuffing," 55, 69, 73, 75, 80, 82, 91-92, 111, 116, 129
Resources/organizations, 25, 42, 163, 175-182
Respite care, 27-29, 36
Resurrection, 88, 154, 159
Revelations/recognitions, 143-146, 148, 153, 157 (*see also* Impressions)
Rituals/ceremonies, 87, 100, 101, 153 (*see also* Funerals)
RTS Bereavement Services, 84, 180

SAD (Seasonal Affective Disorder), 80
Sad/sadness/sorrow, 77, 79, 83-84, 89, 92-94, 96-97, 99, 106, 115, 120, 124, 137, 140, 144-146, 151, 158, 167
Searching/asking why?, 3, 4, 6-9, 12, 17, 20-21, 45, 73, 81, 83-84, 89, 95-97, 104, 128, 131, 133, 138, 153, 167-168, 170
  questions/asking "why?", 114, 116, 119, 120, 139, 145

Secondary loss, 7, 8, 10, 109-110, 120
Seizures, 13, 46, 164-166
Self-defeating behaviors, 57-58
Self-esteem/self-worth, 8, 9, 36, 40-41, 49-66, 64-65, 85-86, 129, 143, 156
Self-help, 9, 79, 98-99, 157
Self-talk, 93
Serotonin/endorphins, 80, 92
Services/programs/treatments, 21, 26-30, 33, 42, 74, 77, 162-163
  home programs, 22, 28, 34, 39, 131
  home exercises, 35
  infant stimulation, 16, 29
  institutional services, 161, 167
  occupational therapy, 29, 33-35, 162
  physical therapy, 19, 22, 29, 32, 34, 39, 52, 65, 131, 162
  residential or group home, 140, 166-167 (*see also* Placement)
Serving others, 42, 73, 86, 89, 94, 97-103, 119-121, 124-125, 130, 134, 158
Sexual intimacy, 112-113, 117
Shock/numbness, 3, 8, 9, 12, 14, 16-17, 70, 72-73, 84, 87, 89, 92, 97, 104, 109, 131, 146
Siblings, 20-21, 41, 49, 57, 96-98, 115, 117-124, 146
Sleep, 13, 30, 39, 60, 62, 65, 72, 78-80, 89, 103, 115, 123, 143, 145, 150, 153, 156, 164
Social needs/society/community, 4, 21, 26, 28, 41, 43, 50, 53, 56, 61, 70, 74, 86-87, 99, 102, 113, 161
  in grief (graph), 71
Speech/vision/hearing, 14, 29, 33-36, 38, 51, 59, 60, 64, 145, 162

Spiritual/religion, 70-73, 87, 95, 97,
    113-114, 118-120, 131-159
    (*see also* Differences)
spiritual healing, 70, 72, 96, 133,
    153-155
spiritual injury in grief, 17, 42,
    72-73, 132-133, 135, 147, 149
    graph, 71
Statistics, 12, 69, 89, 109, 113, 117,
    124, 136, 138, 147, 168-169
Stillborn, 6, 10, 12, 74, 84
Stress, 7, 9, 12, 17, 20, 43, 57, 61,
    80-83, 109, 114, 118, 123
    diagnosis stressors, 69
Suffer/suffering, 46, 56, 74-75,
    84, 87, 89, 96, 106, 115,
    123, 124, 126, 128-129,
    131-133, 147, 157, 166, 168,
    171
Suicide, 4, 5, 9, 10, 52, 77, 103,
    124, 138, 140, 149,
    168-172
and NDEs, 172
Support/support groups, 27, 84-85,
    96-99, 102, 116, 121, 123,
    125, 126, 134
Surgery, 20, 65, 89, 121, 144, 150,
    152, 155, 163

Teens (adolescents), 4, 21, 28, 36,
    38, 40, 52, 60, 61-63, 81,
    111-112, 117-119, 120-121,
    135, 153
puberty, 65
Tests/testing, 12-15, 17, 19, 20-21,
    33, 126, 137, 148, 150, 163
    (*see also* Diagnosis)
TCF (The Compassionate Friends),
    97, 98, 121, 180

Thoughts, 85 [*see also* Positive
    thoughts or attitude;
    Negative (labels) and
    (thoughts); Control;
    Cognitive brain/mind]
Tongue thrust, 14 (*see also* Jaw
    control)
Touch/affection, 82, 102, 111-113,
    117, 118, 119, 123, 132
Toys, 14, 31, 33, 44, 63, 83, 126
Trials (*see* Challenges)
Trust, 113, 118, 119, 123, 132, 159
Truth, 132, 140, 157-158

Value/valued, 46, 53, 55, 58, 65, 89,
    159
Vision (*see* Speech/vision/hearing)
Visions, 141, 144-146, 154
Visitations, 137-138, 140, 144,
    146-147
Visualization, 82

Wishes, 79, 84-85, 112, 122-124,
    141-142, 145-146, 149, 153,
    155
Withdrawal, 19, 20, 86-87, 99, 102,
    119, 127, 133 (*see also*
    Isolation)
Women (*see also* Differences)
characteristics of, 113-117
Worry, 13, 15-18, 20, 26, 39, 45, 59,
    62, 77, 79, 99, 120, 124, 142,
    144, 147-148, 166
Writing (*see* Reading/writing/
    journals)